TSIA2® MASTERY
ELAR

MasteryPrep

Inquiries concerning this publication should be mailed to:

MasteryPrep
7117 Florida Blvd.
Baton Rouge, LA 70806

MasteryPrep is a trade name and/or trademark of Ring Publications LLC.

10 9 8 7 6 5 4 3 2 1

ISBN-13: 978-1-948846-80-6

Table of Contents

Essay

An Introduction to the TSIA2

In this chapter, you will become familiar with the characteristics of the TSIA2 and its rules. Additionally, you will review and evaluate several strategies that can be used to optimize your time and mental energy during their test.

🎯 LEARNING TARGETS

1. Develop a "why" to maintain motivation when preparing for the TSIA2.

2. Identify the minimum scores required to pass each section of the TSIA2.

3. Review how the TSIA2 determines scores.

4. Collect 7 strategies that can be applied during the beginning, middle, and end of the testing period.

 **Groundwork**

EXERCISE A

Instructions

Review the following as your teacher leads the discussion. Then, respond to the prompt in the space provided.

Earning a passing score on the TSIA2 means …

… more money.

… more time.

… being able to support yourself or your family.

… changing your life!

1. What is your "why" for doing well on the TSIA2?

_____

_____

_____

_____

_____

EXERCISE B

Instructions

Fill in the blanks below as your teacher leads the discussion.

Subject	Questions	Score	Passing Score
English Language Arts and Reading			
Multiple Choice	30	910 to 990	
Essay	1	1 to 8	
Mathematics			
Multiple Choice	20	910 to 990	

EXERCISE C

Instructions
Refer to the following diagram as your teacher leads the discussion.

A Map of the TSIA2

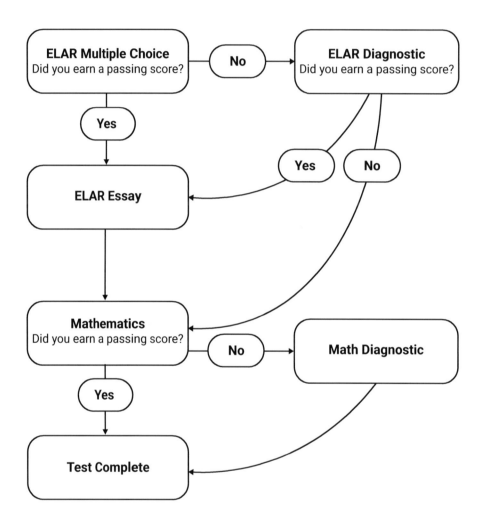

EXERCISE D

Instructions
Draw a line to match each situation to the effect it will have on a person's score as they take a computer-adaptive test.

1. If a student answers several questions correctly,

2. If a student answers several questions incorrectly,

3. If a student answers a single question incorrectly,

4. If a student wants to go back and change an answer,

A. their score may dip slightly.

B. the questions will become more difficult.

C. they should click the "back" button.

D. it's too late. The TSIA2 does not allow students to revisit questions they've already answered.

E. their score will go down more dramatically.

 **Application**

⊘ THE APPROACH

At the beginning of the test, you should ...

1. focus on the early questions.
2. prepare to start with a medium question.

During the middle of the test, you should not ...

3. stress if the questions get harder.
4. overthink because you may just be prepared.

As you get closer to the end of the test, you should ...

5. finish strong.
6. take more mental breaks to avoid getting tired.

During the TSIA2, you should never ...

7. panic!
8. give up if the test gets hard.
9. give up if the questions seem easy.

Instructions

Determine whether each strategy would be helpful during the TSIA2. Put a check mark next to the strategies that you should use.

_____ Take mental breaks if I feel tired or bored.

_____ Go to sleep in the middle of the test.

_____ Reread every question at least 20 times.

_____ Change all of my answers after I've picked them.

_____ Keep focused and push through to the next question as soon as I'm happy with my answer.

Instructions

Identify three things you can change to take ownership of your testing station.

1. _____

2. _____

3. _____

ELAR Orientation

In this chapter, you will learn the ins and outs of the English, Language Arts, and Reading portion of the TSIA2. You will become familiar with the structure and question pattern of the multiple-choice section, as well as gain insight into the rules of the test and minimum scores for passing.

🎯 LEARNING TARGETS

1. Review the structure of the ELAR test of the TSIA2.

2. Recognize five question types that appear on the ELAR test.

3. Evaluate and apply a general strategy that can be applied to all types of reading and writing questions on the TSIA2.

 **Groundwork**

EXERCISE A

Instructions

Refer to the following chart as your teacher leads the discussion.

The English Language Arts and Reading (ELAR) portion of the test has 30 multiple-choice questions and an essay. The two areas of focus for the multiple-choice section of the ELAR test are:

Reading Focus	
Literary Text Analysis	This category includes questions related to the broad concepts of purpose and point of view, as well as specific concepts such as drawing inferences, all in the context of a literary text.
Informational Text Analysis and Synthesis	This category includes organization, word choice, and other composition issues as it relates to an essay.

Writing Focus	
Essay	This category includes organization, word choice, and other composition issues as it relates to an essay.
Sentence	This category includes the conventions of standard written English grammar, punctuation, and spelling within the context of a single sentence.

Instructions

Refer to the following figure and fill in the blanks as your teacher leads the discussion.

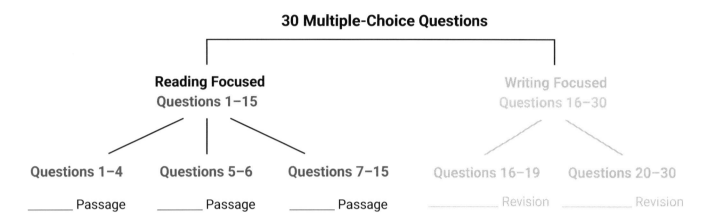

30 Multiple-Choice Questions

Reading Focused
Questions 1–15

Writing Focused
Questions 16–30

Questions 1–4   **Questions 5–6**   **Questions 7–15**   Questions 16–19   Questions 20–30

_____ Passage   _____ Passage   _____ Passage   _____ Revision   _____ Revision

EXERCISE C

Instructions

Refer to the following figure and fill in the blanks as your teacher leads the discussion.

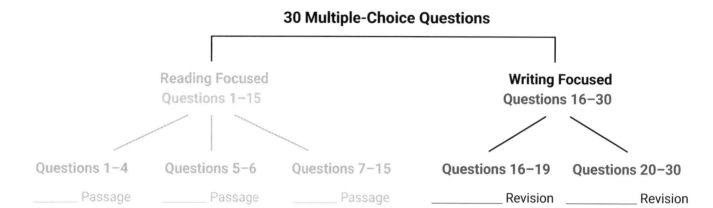

Application

⊘ THE APPROACH

When working on the ELAR portion of the TSIA2, use these steps to answer each question ...

1. Identify the question type.
2. Decode the question.
3. Pick a strategy.
4. Use the process of elimination.

1. To enter the tournament, the student or <u>teacher have to</u> pay $10, and all of the proceeds go to help children with cancer.

    (A) teacher have to

    (B) teacher has to

    (C) teacher must have to

    (D) teacher had to

⊘ THE APPROACH

When working on the ELAR portion of the TSIA2, use these steps to answer each question ...

1. Identify the question type.
2. Decode the question.
3. Pick a strategy.
4. Use the process of elimination.

Passage

In this passage from a novel, the writer describes one man's journey to develop a career as a modern-day philosopher.

Daniel Dennett's eternal search for answers began after his father was killed in an unexplained plane crash. His early life and move from Beirut to Massachusetts was cast in the long shadow of a mythical, unknown father figure. Dennett had come from a family of remarkable brilliance—his father was a counter-intelligence officer in the Office of Strategic Services, a predecessor of the CIA. Dennett attended Harvard University, where he received a doctorate in philosophy. There, he was awarded the prestigious Erasmus prize for his exceptional contribution to society, showcasing how his work was not only important to himself but was also significant within a worldwide community.

During Dennett's first year at Winchester High School, he put all his effort into a term paper on Plato and included a picture of Rodin's *The Thinker* on the cover. He humorously recalled that at the time, he hadn't really understood a word of what he had written. At age seventeen, he had begun pursuing a mathematics degree at Wesleyan University and found himself drowning in his coursework. Studying in the library late one evening, he happened upon the text *From a Logical Point of View*, which had been written at Harvard University by Willard Van Orman Quine. He was utterly transfixed, and by the next morning he had made up his mind to transfer to Harvard.

At the end of his college career, Dennett had begun developing his own thoughts and contradicting the opinions of philosophers who came before him. By 1962, he was twenty and married and could no longer relate to the idyllic days of his youth. He was experiencing for the first time a voracious drive to refute Quine's work. His youthful misguidance had now been given purpose. He chose to follow the path of questioning established truths, and regardless of the daunting complexities involved, he was coming up with His Own Answers. Now there was no turning back; he was the one calling the shots. In his thesis defense, he was so convincing that an established professor defended one of his critiques of Quine against the objectives of another faculty member. This remarkable affirmation inspired in him true self-confidence, and Dennett went on to build an academic career asking poignant questions.

2. The details describing Dennett's father in the first paragraph are most likely included to

   Ⓐ explain that Dennett felt an urge to follow in his father's footsteps

   Ⓑ demonstrate the legacy of intelligence Dennett was born into

   Ⓒ suggest that Dennett's father's military career was similar to that of Dennett's in academia

   Ⓓ show that few philosophers relate to growing up in a military household

Instructions

Use the provided space to take notes as your teacher leads the discussion.

Notes

_____

_____

_____

_____

_____

_____

_____

_____

_____

_____

_____

_____

_____

This page is intentionally left blank.
Content resumes on the next page.

Long Passages

In this chapter, you will evaluate the characteristics of a long passage question from the TSIA2. In addition, you will review and apply a strategy that can be used to answer any TSIA2 question with those characteristics.

🎯 LEARNING TARGETS

1. Identify the characteristics of a long passage question.

2. Utilize a prescribed strategy to eliminate incorrect answer choices.

Groundwork

EXERCISE A

Instructions

Refer to the following question as your teacher leads the discussion. Do not answer the question.

In this passage from a novel, the writer describes one man's journey to develop a career as a modern-day philosopher.

Passage

Daniel Dennett's eternal search for answers began after his father was killed in an unexplained plane crash. His early life and move from Beirut to Massachusetts were cast in the long shadow of a mythical, unknown father figure. Dennett had come from a family of remarkable brilliance—his father was a counterintelligence officer in the Office of Strategic Services, a predecessor of the CIA. Dennett attended Harvard University, where he received a doctorate in philosophy. There he was awarded the prestigious Erasmus prize for his exceptional contribution to society, showcasing how his work was not only important to himself but was also significant within a worldwide community.

During Dennett's first year at Winchester High School, he put all his effort into a term paper on Plato and included a picture of Rodin's *The Thinker* on the cover. He humorously recalled that at the time, he hadn't really understood a word of what he had written. At age seventeen, he had begun pursuing a mathematics degree at Wesleyan University and found himself drowning in his coursework. Studying in the library late one evening, he chanced upon the text From a Logical Point of View, which had been written at Harvard University by Willard Van Orman Quine. He was utterly transfixed, and by the next morning, he had made up his mind to transfer to Harvard.

At the end of his college career, Dennett had begun developing his own thoughts and contradicting the opinions of philosophers who came before him. By 1962 he was twenty and married and could no longer relate to the idyllic days of his youth. He was experiencing for the first time a voracious drive to refute Quine's work. His youthful misguidance had now been given purpose. The pursuit of a valuable quarry through daunting complexities was the path he had chosen to follow, and regardless of the ambiguity of right and wrong, he was coming up with His Own Answers. Now that there was no turning back, he was the one calling the shots. He defended his thesis well and had so convinced others of his points that an established professor defended a point of contention that Dennett argued against Quine. The remarkable affirmation inspired in him true self-confidence, and Dennett went on to build an academic career asking poignant questions.

1. The main purpose of the passage is to

    (A) propose that by following the steps taken by Dennett, others can become philosophers as well

    (B) persuade the reader that Dennett was only able to ask questions no one could answer

    (C) speculate on how philosophers employ different methods to approach an argument

    (D) describe how Dennett developed from an inexperienced student into an established philosopher

EXERCISE B

Instructions
Review the basic steps for answering a long passage question. Put them into the correct sequence by filling in numbers 1–5 in the spaces provided.

_____ Find the big picture.

_____ Read the passage first.

_____ Read the question.

_____ Find your evidence.

_____ Use the process of elimination.

Application

⊘ THE APPROACH

When answering a long passage question on the TSIA2, use these steps ...

1. Read the passage first.
2. Read the question.
3. Find the big picture.
4. Find your evidence.
5. Use the process of elimination.

In this passage from a novel, the writer describes one man's journey to develop a career as a modern-day philosopher.

Passage

Daniel Dennett's eternal search for answers began after his father was killed in an unexplained plane crash. His early life and move from Beirut to Massachusetts were cast in the long shadow of a mythical, unknown father figure. Dennett had come from a family of remarkable brilliance—his father was a counterintelligence officer in the Office of Strategic Services, a predecessor of the CIA. Dennett attended Harvard University, where he received a doctorate in philosophy. There he was awarded the prestigious Erasmus prize for his exceptional contribution to society, showcasing how his work was not only important to himself but was also significant within a worldwide community.

During Dennett's first year at Winchester High School, he put all his effort into a term paper on Plato and included a picture of Rodin's *The Thinker* on the cover. He humorously recalled that at the time, he hadn't really understood a word of what he had written. At age seventeen, he had begun pursuing a mathematics degree at Wesleyan University and found himself drowning in his coursework. Studying in the library late one evening, he chanced upon the text From a Logical Point of View, which had been written at Harvard University by Willard Van Orman Quine. He was utterly transfixed, and by the next morning, he had made up his mind to transfer to Harvard.

At the end of his college career, Dennett had begun developing his own thoughts and contradicting the opinions of philosophers who came before him. By 1962 he was twenty and married and could no longer relate to the idyllic days of his youth. He was experiencing for the first time a voracious drive to refute Quine's work. His youthful misguidance had now been given purpose. The pursuit of a valuable quarry through daunting complexities was the path he had chosen to follow, and regardless of the ambiguity of right and wrong, he was coming up with His Own Answers. Now that there was no turning back, he was the one calling the shots. He defended his thesis well and had so convinced others of his points that an established professor defended a point of contention that Dennett argued against Quine. The remarkable affirmation inspired in him true self-confidence, and Dennett went on to build an academic career asking poignant questions.

1. The main purpose of the passage is to

   Ⓐ propose that by following the steps taken by Dennett, others can become philosophers as well

   Ⓑ persuade the reader that Dennett was only able to ask questions no one could answer

   Ⓒ speculate on how philosophers employ different methods to approach an argument

   Ⓓ describe how Dennett developed from an inexperienced student into an established philosopher

⊘ THE APPROACH

When answering a long passage question on the TSIA2, use these steps ...

1. Read the passage first.
2. Read the question.
3. Find the big picture.
4. Find your evidence.
5. Use the process of elimination.

In this passage from a novel, the writer describes one man's journey to develop a career as a modern-day philosopher.

Passage

Daniel Dennett's eternal search for answers began after his father was killed in an unexplained plane crash. His early life and move from Beirut to Massachusetts were cast in the long shadow of a mythical, unknown father figure. Dennett had come from a family of remarkable brilliance—his father was a counterintelligence officer in the Office of Strategic Services, a predecessor of the CIA. Dennett attended Harvard University, where he received a doctorate in philosophy. There he was awarded the prestigious Erasmus prize for his exceptional contribution to society, showcasing how his work was not only important to himself but was also significant within a worldwide community.

During Dennett's first year at Winchester High School, he put all his effort into a term paper on Plato and included a picture of Rodin's *The Thinker* on the cover. He humorously recalled that at the time, he hadn't really understood a word of what he had written. At age seventeen, he had begun pursuing a mathematics degree at Wesleyan University and found himself drowning in his coursework. Studying in the library late one evening, he chanced upon the text From a Logical Point of View, which had been written at Harvard University by Willard Van Orman Quine. He was utterly transfixed, and by the next morning, he had made up his mind to transfer to Harvard.

At the end of his college career, Dennett had begun developing his own thoughts and contradicting the opinions of philosophers who came before him. By 1962 he was twenty and married and could no longer relate to the idyllic days of his youth. He was experiencing for the first time a voracious drive to refute Quine's work. His youthful misguidance had now been given purpose. The pursuit of a valuable quarry through daunting complexities was the path he had chosen to follow, and regardless of the ambiguity of right and wrong, he was coming up with His Own Answers. Now that there was no turning back, he was the one calling the shots. He defended his thesis well and had so convinced others of his points that an established professor defended a point of contention that Dennett argued against Quine. The remarkable affirmation inspired in him true self-confidence, and Dennett went on to build an academic career asking poignant questions.

2. The main purpose of the second paragraph is to

   Ⓐ describe a specific text written by Dennett's rival, Quine

   Ⓑ present the process students undertake to defend their philosophical theses

   Ⓒ provide an account of Dennett's transformation from youth to maturity

   Ⓓ list several ways Dennett contradicted the teachings of his mentors

 **Practice**

Instructions
Complete the practice set. If time remains after you've finished, double-check your work.

The narrator of this passage, excerpted from an essay, describes the life of a pet dog.

Passage
The day he came was a beautiful, bright, cool one in August. A touring car brought him. They put him down on our corner, meaning to lose him, but he crawled under the car, and they had to prod him out and throw stones before they could drive on. I carried him over the railroad tracks. That night he got chop bones and slept on the mat. The second morning we thought he had gone. The third he was back, wagging approval of us and intent to stay, which seemed to leave no choice but to take him in. We had fun over names: "Jellywaggles," "Rags," or "Toby." Finally, we called him "Nibbie," and soon, his tail would answer to it.

Cleaned up—scrubbed, the insoluble matted locks clipped from his coat, his trampish collar replaced with a new one bearing a license tag—he was far from being unpresentable. Always, depending on the moment's mood, he was either terrier or spaniel, the snap and scrap and perk of the one alternating with the gentle snuggling indolence of the other.

As a terrier, he would dig furiously by the hour after a field mouse; as a spaniel, he would "read" the breeze with the best nose among the dog folk of our neighborhood or follow a trail quite well. I know there was retrieving blood. A year ago in May, he caught and brought me, not doing the least injury, an oriole that probably had flown against a wire and was struggling disabled in the grass.

Nibbie was shabby-genteel black, sunburnt as to the mustache, grizzled as to the raggy fringe on his haunches. He had a white stock and shirt frill and a white forepaw. The brown eyes full of heart was the best point. His body coat was rough Scottish worsted, the little black pate was cotton-soft like shoddy, and the big black ears were genuine spaniel silk. As a terrier, he held them up smartly and carried a plumy fishhook of a tail; as a spaniel, the ears drooped, and the tail swung meekly as if in apology for never having been clipped. In flea time, it seemed hardly possible that a dog of his size could sustain his population. We finally found a true fleabane, but deserted one day, and he was populous again the next.

1. In describing Nibbie's problem with fleas and the doubt that Nibbie could "sustain his population," the narrator is most directly referring to the fact that

    (A) the fleas living on Nibbie made him afraid to leave the clothes-closet to eat his dinner

    (B) Nibbie wagged his tail at the family but snapped blindly at fleas when left alone

    (C) no other dog in the neighborhood had as many fleas as Nibbie had that season

    (D) the large number of fleas living on Nibbie was incongruous to his small size

2. When the author says that Nibbie's first owners let him out, "meaning to lose him," he most likely means

    (A) the first owners were careless and could not keep track of him.

    (B) Nibbie's owners were abandoning him.

    (C) Nibbie wandered off and got lost.

    (D) the author lost Nibbie under the car.

3. When the author writes that Nibbie was "retrieving blood," he most likely means that he

    (A) was a ferocious hunter that brought back his kills to the narrator

    (B) had a health problem involving his blood vessels

    (C) sustained a gruesome injury while playing fetch

    (D) displayed characteristics of a particular breed of dog

This page is intentionally left blank.
Content resumes on the next page.

Vocabulary

In this chapter, you will practice a process for evaluating the connotation and denotation of specific vocabulary words in the context of a passage. You will learn a process for identifying context clues and determining the proper definitions through logical reasoning.

🎯 LEARNING TARGETS

1. Evaluate how context influences the definition of a word.

2. Develop a definition for a word based on how it is used in a passage.

3. Utilize the features of the test to eliminate incorrect answers.

 **Warm-Up**

Instructions
Complete the warm-up question. If time remains after you've finished, double-check your work.

Passage
(1) Have you ever had the chance to look at the map of a person's heart? (2) Science textbooks sometimes include different kinds of diagrams of the heart, and its crisscrossing ventricles can be fascinating, but see them try to draw a map of a child's heart, which is not merely disorganized, but always changing direction. (3) Its lines go up and down, just like a heart rhythm on a monitor, and these are likely paths in the forest, for the Evermore is always generally speaking a forest, with dazzling flecks of light here and there, and vines and rusted-over carts in the brush, silent caves, and elves who are usually carpenters, and bridges under which a creek passes, princesses who are the eldest of five sisters, and a shack slowly being lost to ruin, and one large old man with a cleft chin. (4) If that were it, it would form a simple map, but there are also first birthday parties, classrooms, mothers, the babbling brook, stitching, thefts, executions, nouns of the third declension, frosted cupcake day, getting a retainer, write four plus three, a nickel for a tooth under your pillow, and so on, and either these are an aspect of the forest or they reveal another map peeking out, and it is all quite disorienting, especially because nothing remains still.

(5) Naturally the Evermores differ quite a bit. (6) Alex's, for instance, has a bog with bald eagles gliding over it at which Alex was aiming, while Jack, who was still little, had a bald eagle with bogs gliding over it. (7) Alex lived in a bus flipped sideways in the undergrowth, Jack in a teepee, Mary in a hut of carefully sculpted clay. (8) Alex didn't have friends, Jack had friends only at night, and Mary had a pet snake cast away by its parents, but for the most part the Evermores display a family resemblance, and if they lined up side by side you wouldn't be wrong to say they had each other's eyes, and so on. (9) On these enchanted paths kids at play are for ever mounting their buckboards. (10) We too have journeyed there; we still can hear the crunching of leaves, though we shall steer its grounds no more.

(11) Of all the tantalizing forests the Evermore is the coziest and most compact, not wide and ranging, you see, with tiresome stretches between one adventure and the next, but nicely packed. (12) When visiting by day in games with tables and teacups, it isn't alarming in the least, but come the minute before the lights go out, it all becomes quite real. (13) That is the reason for bed lamps.

1. In sentence 10, "we" most likely refers to

   Ⓐ authors

   Ⓑ kids

   Ⓒ believers

   Ⓓ adults

 **Groundwork**

EXERCISE A

Instructions

Review the following list of words:

- Pirate
- Ship
- Treasure
- Raid
- Lookout

1. What book, movie, or character comes to mind? _____

EXERCISE B

Instructions
Refer to the following passage as your teacher leads the discussion.

Passage
My brother called to tell me he would **ship** my birthday present so I would be on the **lookout** for it. Although I watched the tracking number online, porch **pirates** **raided** my home before I could get there to pick up my packages. Luckily, my video doorbell caught them. Amazingly, the police retrieved my packages, including my birthday present. I will always **treasure** the handmade scarf my brother sent.

2. Was the passage what you expected? Circle your answer.

Yes   No

EXERCISE C

Instructions
Read the following passage and use its contents to answer the questions below.

Passage
    The members of the debate team were recruited from the high schools with the highest-ranked programs in the state. At first, the recruits were thrilled to have the opportunity to train with Mr. Sullivan, or "Sully," who was one of the top debate coaches in the country. But they soon realized that working with Sully was no walk in the park. He was meticulous to the point of exacting, and recruits started **dropping**; they were not willing to put up with Sully's criticisms of their efforts. Before long, there were only six of the original fifteen team members remaining. Rather than seeming upset by the diminished size of his team, though, Sully seemed satisfied.

3.   Underline the nearby words that give you hints about the meaning of the word "dropping."

4.   Write your own definition for the word "dropping."

_____

_____

Application

⊘ THE APPROACH

When a question asks you to identify what a word means or refers to, use the following steps ...

1. Read the word in context.
2. Develop your own definition.
3. Select the answer that best matches what you came up with.

Instructions

Read the passage below and then choose the best answer to each question. Answer the questions on the basis of what is <u>stated</u> or <u>implied</u> in the passage.

Passage

(1) It was the very witching time of night that Ichabod, heavy-hearted and crestfallen, pursued his travels homewards, along the sides of the lofty hills which rise above Tarry Town, and which he had traversed so cheerily in the afternoon. **(2)** The hour was as dismal as himself. **(3)** Far below him, the Tappan Zee spread its dusky and indistinct waste of waters, with here and there the tall mast of a sloop, riding quietly at anchor under the land. **(4)** In the dead hush of midnight, he could even hear the barking of the watch-dog from the opposite shore of the Hudson; but it was so vague and faint as only to give an idea of his distance from this faithful companion of man.

From Washington Irving, *The Legend of Sleepy Hollow*.

5. In sentence 1, the word "pursued" most nearly means

   Ⓐ chased after
   Ⓑ proceeded with
   Ⓒ strived for
   Ⓓ haunted

⊘ THE APPROACH

When a question asks you to identify what a word means or refers to, use the following steps ...

1. Read the word in context.
2. Develop your own definition.
3. Select the answer that best matches what you came up with.

Instructions

Read the passage below and then choose the best answer to each question. Answer the questions on the basis of what is <u>stated</u> or <u>implied</u> in the passage.

Passage

(1) All the stories of ghosts and goblins that he had heard in the afternoon now came crowding upon his recollection. **(2)** The night grew darker and darker; the stars seemed to sink deeper in the sky, and driving clouds occasionally hid them from his sight. **(3)** He had never felt so lonely and dismal. **(4)** He was, moreover, approaching the very place where many of the scenes of the ghost stories had been laid. **(5)** In the center of the road stood an enormous tulip-tree, which towered like a giant above all the other trees of the neighborhood, and formed a kind of landmark. . . . **(6)** It was connected with the tragical story of the unfortunate André, who had been taken prisoner hard by; and was universally known by the name of Major André's tree.

(7) As he approached the stream, his heart began to thump. . . . **(8)** In the dark shadow of the grove, on the margin of the brook, he beheld something huge, misshapen, black, and towering. **(9)** It stirred not, but seemed gathered up in the gloom, like some gigantic monster ready to spring upon the traveler. . . . **(10)** He appeared to be a horseman of large dimensions, and mounted on a black horse of powerful frame. **(11)** He made no offer of molestation or sociability, but kept aloof on one side of the road, jogging along on the blind side of old Gunpowder. **(12)** Ichabod now quickened his steed, in hopes of leaving him behind. **(13)** The stranger, however, quickened his horse to an equal pace. **(14)** Ichabod pulled up, and fell into a walk, thinking to lag behind—the other did the same.

From Washington Irving, *The Legend of Sleepy Hollow*.

6. In sentence 4, the word "laid" refers to where the ghost stories were

   Ⓐ said to have happened
   Ⓑ buried beneath the ground
   Ⓒ written by the storyteller
   Ⓓ given new life each year

 **Practice**

Instructions
Complete the practice set. If time remains after you've finished, double-check your work.

Passage
    If you've ever experienced a slight burning or tingly sensation when eating pineapple, you're not alone. The reason is bromelain, an enzyme found in pineapple that is then easily digested in your stomach. Unfortunately, before reaching your stomach, bromelain breaks down the proteins on your tongue, which the body discerns as an attack. As a result, pineapple can be slightly painful to eat while being perfectly harmless to digestion.

1. The word "discerns" in sentence 3 of the passage most nearly means

    (A) imagines

    (B) produces

    (C) anticipates

    (D) interprets

Passage
    Incensed by civil and economic injustices in 1786, farmers in rural Massachusetts planned attacks on government forces. This insurrection became known as Shays' Rebellion. In 1787, after militia commander William Shepherd's forces were deemed too small to oppose the growing insurrection, Governor John Bowdoin ordered that a private militia be formed to quash the rebellion. Although only a fraction of the 4,000 rebels were jailed (later to be freed), Shays' Rebellion showed that the new government formed under the Articles of Confederation did not have the resources to suppress violent uprisings against its laws.

2. As used in sentence 3, the word "quash" most nearly means

    (A) complete

    (B) release

    (C) protect

    (D) suppress

Passage

During the process of anaerobic digestion, animal waste produces methane gas. Recently, biochemists sponsored by the Department of Energy discovered a way to make synthetic versions of waste that give off even more methane. You might be asking why the Department of Energy is sponsoring such developments. The reason is that methane produced by such waste could someday generate enough electricity for a whole city.

3. As used in sentence 2, the word "synthetic" means

   (A) powerful

   (B) manufactured

   (C) ineffective

   (D) safe

Wrap-Up

Instructions
Complete the wrap-up question. If time remains after you've finished, double-check your work.

Passage
(1) Have you ever had the chance to look at the map of a person's heart? (2) Science textbooks sometimes include different kinds of diagrams of the heart, and its crisscrossing ventricles can be fascinating, but see them try to draw a map of a child's heart, which is not merely disorganized, but always changing direction. (3) Its lines go up and down, just like a heart rhythm on a monitor, and these are likely paths in the forest, for the Evermore is always generally speaking a forest, with dazzling flecks of light here and there, and vines and rusted-over carts in the brush, silent caves, and elves who are usually carpenters, and bridges under which a creek passes, princesses who are the eldest of five sisters, and a shack slowly being lost to ruin, and one large old man with a cleft chin. (4) If that were it, it would form a simple map, but there are also first birthday parties, classrooms, mothers, the babbling brook, stitching, thefts, executions, nouns of the third declension, frosted cupcake day, getting a retainer, write four plus three, a nickel for a tooth under your pillow, and so on, and either these are an aspect of the forest or they reveal another map peeking out, and it is all quite disorienting, especially because nothing remains still.

(5) Naturally the Evermores differ quite a bit. (6) Alex's, for instance, has a bog with bald eagles gliding over it at which Alex was aiming, while Jack, who was still little, had a bald eagle with bogs gliding over it. (7) Alex lived in a bus flipped sideways in the undergrowth, Jack in a teepee, Mary in a hut of carefully sculpted clay. (8) Alex didn't have friends, Jack had friends only at night, and Mary had a pet snake cast away by its parents, but for the most part the Evermores display a family resemblance, and if they lined up side by side you wouldn't be wrong to say they had each other's eyes, and so on. (9) On these enchanted paths kids at play are for ever mounting their buckboards. (10) We too have journeyed there; we still can hear the crunching of leaves, though we shall steer its grounds no more.

(11) Of all the tantalizing forests the Evermore is the coziest and most compact, not wide and ranging, you see, with tiresome stretches between one adventure and the next, but nicely packed. (12) When visiting by day in games with tables and teacups, it isn't alarming in the least, but come the minute before the lights go out, it all becomes quite real. (13) That is the reason for bed lamps.

2. In sentence 8, the reference to "eyes" most likely represents

  (A) a frequent sight in Evermores

  (B) shared characteristics among siblings

  (C) omens from children's nightmares

  (D) differences among varying Evermores

Main Idea

In this chapter, you will be tasked with reviewing the details of a passage, locating key words and phrases, and identifying the main idea.

🎯 **LEARNING TARGETS**

1. Identify the topic of a passage.

2. Evaluate details of a passage to determine its main idea.

3. Utilize features of the passage, such as the topic sentence, to aid in the process of elimination.

Warm-Up

Instructions

Complete the warm-up question. If time remains after you've finished, double-check your work.

Passage

The Statue of Liberty is one of the most recognizable symbols of American liberty, but on occasion it has come close to losing its signature torch. Shortly after the light first debuted in New York City in 1886, it burned out as it was being tested. The light was repaired; however, it burned out again 12 years later. Finally, as the light shone in 1918 in honor of the end of World War I, it burned out again—damaging the existing torch so much that the whole fixture had to be replaced.

1. The passage is mainly concerned with

    (A) the creation of the Statue of Liberty

    (B) the celebration of the end of World War I

    (C) the problems with the Statue of Liberty's torch

    (D) important symbols of independence in the United States

Groundwork

EXERCISE A

Instructions

Read each list of words. Then, create a title for each based on your analysis. Write it in the space provided.

1. _____	2. _____
springtime	Spanish
holiday	Hmong
jokes	Creole
pranks	Mandarin
the 1st	Arabic

EXERCISE B

Instructions

Read the passage and underline the key words. Use those key words to create a title for this passage. Write your answer in the space provided.

Passage

3. _____

   The concept of a "good luck" charm is found in almost every culture on the planet. You're probably familiar with the more common good luck charms, like a four-leaf clover or rabbit's foot. Others are lesser-known. For instance, ancient sailors thought dolphins were lucky because seeing them meant land was likely close by. Vikings were particularly fond of acorns as symbols of good luck. This is linked to their god of thunder, Thor, and how often lightning struck oak trees. Vikings would collect the acorns and keep them in their pocket or windowsill as a way to protect themselves. Yet another example comes from the Navajo tribes. If a dragonfly landed on you, it was considered a lucky omen proving that you would recover from any hardship you'd been suffering through.

Application

⊘ THE APPROACH

When you are asked to find the main idea of a paragraph or passage, use these steps …

1. Locate key words in the passage.
2. Identify the passage's topic.
3. Eliminate answer choices that don't match the passage's topic.

Passage

When a person hopes for a good outcome, they often perform a simple gesture: crossing their fingers. But, where does this practice come from? What impact could intertwining one's digits have on an outcome in the real world? The truth of the matter is that no one is exactly sure why we do this. One theory stems from yet another practice: when individuals would make a wish, someone would offer "support" by laying their finger across the other's to help the wish come true. Another possible origin is the Pagan belief that spirits often dwell near crossroads. By crossing fingers, a person could essentially create their own "crossroad," drawing in good luck from the spirits. Despite its unclear origins, the practice of crossing fingers for good luck persists well into today's world.

4. This passage is mainly about

   Ⓐ how often people cross their fingers

   Ⓑ people crossing their fingers in today's world

   Ⓒ the reason people cross their fingers

   Ⓓ how people wished for good luck in the past

⊘ THE APPROACH

When you are asked to find the main idea of a paragraph or passage, use these steps ...

1. Locate key words in the passage.
2. Identify the passage's topic.
3. Eliminate answer choices that don't match the passage's topic.

Passage

In Lopburi, Thailand, the macaques—a unique primate native to the area—have their very own celebration, which is enough to intrigue even the most skeptical of travelers. On the final Sunday of every November, locals put out a massive banquet, comprised of watermelons, durian, pineapple, dragonfruit, and a number of other sweet indulgences for the monkeys. This practice dates back more than 2,000 years and is a celebration of the monkey King Hanuman and the aid he provided the divine prince Rama. Naturally, this spectacle draws tourists every year. However, once the food runs out, the macaques tend to get a bit unruly and often lash out at spectators. For this reason, it's a good idea to leave well before the tables are emptied.

5. What is the author's main purpose?

   (A) To offer readers an interesting tourist destination
   (B) To explain why tourists are often in danger during this event
   (C) To point out the location of a unique yearly celebration
   (D) To contrast the legends of two cultural deities

 **Practice**

Instructions
Complete the practice set. If time remains after you've finished, double-check your work.

Passage
The Granary Burying Ground in Boston, Massachusetts, is where you can find the tombs of thousands of Bostonians, many of whom played major roles in the American Revolution. John Hancock, the statesman and famous signer of the Declaration, was laid to rest there in 1793, and the patriot Paul Revere followed him in 1818. The graveyard quickly became one of the city's most visited tourist attractions. According to historical documents, the two most-frequented sites in the whole state in 1900 were Boston Common and the adjacent Granary Burying Ground.

1. What is the author's main purpose?

    Ⓐ To present to readers an interesting site to see

    Ⓑ To describe why a burial ground gets so many tourists

    Ⓒ To point out the final resting place of two significant Bostonians

    Ⓓ To contrast two famous sightseeing destinations

Passage
American inventor Thomas Edison is thought by most physics historians to have been the first to functionally use the power of electricity, and his 1878 invention of the lightbulb is legendary. Nevertheless, many Italians think of their native son Alessandro Volta, not Edison, as the first to successfully harness electricity. One day in 1800, according to his assistants' accounts, Volta set up an electric circuit, connected his battery, and produced a brief current. Volta could not generate a strong or constant charge, but he achieved something nonetheless.

2. What is the passage primarily discussing?

    Ⓐ The accomplishment of Alessandro Volta

    Ⓑ The difficulties in early electrical discoveries

    Ⓒ The first use of electricity in the United States

    Ⓓ The story of long-range electricity use

Passage

Just downslope from its source in the Rocky Mountains, near the La Poudre Pass Lake, the Colorado River is almost 2 miles above sea level. However, elsewhere there are long stretches of the river, as it nears its mouth (the Gulf of California), where the Colorado is a mere 100 feet above sea level.

3. The passage is mainly discussing the Colorado River's

Ⓐ depth

Ⓑ length

Ⓒ elevation

Ⓓ location

 Wrap-Up

Instructions
Complete the wrap-up question. If time remains after you've finished, double-check your work.

Passage
Guam is an island territory of the United States located along the western edge of the Mariana Trench in the Pacific Ocean. Given Guam's history as a colony of Spain and its political situation—it is an unincorporated territory of the United States—one might think that the name "Guam" is of Spanish or English origin. However, "Guam" is actually derived from the Chamorro phrase *Guahan*, meaning "we have," the greeting given to Spanish sailors by fruit sellers from the Chamorro tribe, a group that settled the island almost 4,000 years ago.

2. This passage is mainly about

- Ⓐ how Guam got its name
- Ⓑ where Guam is located
- Ⓒ who governs Guam
- Ⓓ what happened to Guam in the past

This page is intentionally left blank.
Content resumes on the next page.

Author's Craft

In this chapter, you will analyze elements of a text to determine how they contribute to the author's purpose.

🎯 LEARNING TARGETS

1. Identify the purpose of a passage.

2. Assess how different types of details work to support a text's purpose.

Warm-Up

Instructions
Complete the warm-up question. If time remains after you've finished, double-check your work.

Passage
   Dubai, UAE, is designing the world's first indoor town, a 4,500-square-kilometer development including hotels, shops, entertainment and health centers, and even an indoor ski slope. The Mall of the World, as the project is called, will be eco-friendly. Lush vegetation will be cultivated under a glass dome that encloses the "town," with conifer forests providing natural air filtration. And, a canopy of solar panels will produce electricity, provide shade, and power automobiles for the residents.

1.   The author refers to vegetation and solar panels in order to

   (A)   introduce a new topic

   (B)   counter an argument

   (C)   criticize a proposal

   (D)   support a claim

 **Groundwork**

EXERCISE A

Instructions
Identify the likely purpose of each of the books described below. Circle your answer.

1. *A Man, a Plan, a Canal, Panama: The Case against Roosevelt*

    Should Roosevelt be seen as the hero of the Panama Canal? This book argues that the commanding engineers on the ground in Panama should get the credit history gives Theodore Roosevelt.

    To Inform   To Entertain   To Persuade

2. *My Quest for Freedom in the Desert*

    A historical fiction novel illustrates the protagonist's thrilling adventures while surviving two years in the Sahara Desert, from fleeing life-or-death danger to discovering hidden miracles.

    To Inform   To Entertain   To Persuade

3. *Silent Islands: The Decline of the Hawaiian Songbird*

    This historical description charts the extinction of many native Hawaiian bird species and explains how the loss of these species can affect ecosystems around the world.

    To Inform   To Entertain   To Persuade

EXERCISE B

Instructions
Determine the purpose of the underlined sentence in the passage below.

Passage
(1) The animal overpasses and underpasses on the Trans-Canada Highway have reduced large animal-vehicle deaths by almost 100 percent. (2) Unfortunately, animals are not as well protected along Canada's railways. (3) <u>Since they have been so successful with the highway programs, wildlife officials should also work with the railways to provide crossings for animals.</u> (4) The direct result of wildlife death in a train-animal collision is only part of the problem. (5) An animal carcass will attract other animals to the railroad tracks. (6) Furthermore, spilled grains and other food products bring animals to the railroad tracks, increasing the likelihood of collisions.

criticize an idea	provide evidence	support a claim	offer a counterargument

4. The purpose of sentence (3) is to _____.

EXERCISE C

Instructions
Match each underlined detail with a purpose suggested in the bank below.

Passage
(7) Due to the high number of animal deaths leading to problems in the genetic pool of wildlife, it would be worth the expense to create bridges and fences to funnel wildlife over railroad tracks in high traffic areas. (8) <u>The railroads, however, are privately owned, and therefore do not have to support government projects.</u> (9) Railroad company owners note that the high costs of fencing and overpasses would severely deplete their profits. (10) <u>But it doesn't have to be this way: to combat the high costs of overpasses, Sweden is experimenting with fencing that guides animals to special crosswalks.</u> (11) Before a train approaches, an alarm (like hunting dogs barking) sounds to frighten the animals off the track, and the sound is reinforced by the train speeding by. (12) <u>This method is much lower in cost than overpasses since the main expense is installing fencing, around 50,000 euros per 50 kilometers.</u> (13) A broader application of these methods would likely prove worthwhile for railroads, their clients, and local wildlife alike.

criticize an idea	provide evidence	support a claim	offer a counterargument

5. The purpose of sentence **(8)** is to _____.

6. The purpose of sentence **(10)** is to _____.

7. The purpose of sentence **(12)** is to _____.

Application

⊘ THE APPROACH

When asked to identify the purpose of a detail in a passage, use the following steps ...

1. Locate and review the target detail.
2. Evaluate the surrounding context of the detail.
3. Eliminate answers that do not correctly describe the detail's purpose.

Passage

In some locales, wildlife overpasses and underpasses are designed specifically for the kinds of wildlife that need them. In Amherst, Massachusetts, wildlife professionals built tunnels for spotted salamanders to cross under city streets. In Powys, Wales, the city council designed ditches and tunnels to lead toads to their breeding grounds and keep them off the roads. In Kenya, there is even an underpass for elephants. On Christmas Island, in Australia, red crabs migrate to the beach to breed, often crossing highways and roads. To protect this flood of creatures, wildlife biologists and civil engineers have designed crab tunnels and crab bridges to funnel the crabs to the beaches and keep them off the roads.

8. The author includes details about red crab breeding grounds in order to

   Ⓐ describe an example
   Ⓑ criticize an argument
   Ⓒ present a solution
   Ⓓ introduce a new topic

⊘ THE APPROACH

When asked to identify the purpose of a detail in a passage, use the following steps ...

1. Locate and review the target detail.
2. Evaluate the surrounding context of the detail.
3. Eliminate answers that do not correctly describe the detail's purpose.

Passage

It is clear that these overpasses and underpasses are amazingly successful. There are approximately one million animal-car collisions each year. These crashes usually kill the animal that is involved, resulting in up to a million large animal deaths due to vehicles per year. A car will kill a small animal with little to no damage to the car. However, a collision with a deer can cause an average of $8,000 of damage to cars, while an impact with a moose or camel is likely to completely destroy a car and possibly kill the driver. However, when a wildlife crossing is constructed, and the animals learn to use it, the rate of animal-vehicle collisions decreases by 85–90%. The increase in safety to motorists and the protection of wildlife would make these crossings a worthy financial investment for any district.

9. The author includes $8,000 of damage and 85–90% improvements in order to

   (A) underscore the benefits of building wildlife crossings to decrease road hazards
   (B) suggest that the cost of animal-vehicle collisions is much less than the cost of the crossings
   (C) explain that wildlife crossings are not completely infallible
   (D) reiterate that the cost of damage is nothing in comparison to the lost lives of deer

 **Practice**

Instructions

Complete the practice set. If time remains after you've finished, double-check your work.

Passage

The narrator of this passage from a novel is a teenage girl from the United States who now lives in France. She and her friend Inès are setting out to find a manuscript that may or may not be real.

(1) That name, *Catacombes de Paris*. **(2)** It could mean more than a subterranean network of tunnels. **(3)** It could also refer to the complex interrelationships of the city itself: the crossroads of Paris. **(4)** There's adventure in that name, and mystery. **(5)** It's an intersection, a bridge to the afterlife, a place just underfoot. **(6)** The air felt as heavy with secrecy as it was with the smell of earth, with whispers, with mold.

(7) There were other memorable names to be found within the tunnels themselves: the *Sarcophagus of Lacrymatoire*, the *Fountain of the Samaritan*, their titles evocative of antiquity and myth, located in the bowels of the tunnels. **(8)** Looky-loos laden with cameras around their necks and guidebooks in hand hustled through the entrance, eager to make their own finds. **(9)** They talked loudly about the hidden treasures they expected to encounter as if their confidence might actually help locate them. **(10)** The Sepulchral Lamp. **(11)** The Atelier. **(12)** The Crypt of Sacellum.

(13) Inès had left to buy tickets. **(14)** I waited patiently by the entrance, scarcely believing that we were really going through with this but not quite nervous. **(15)** If we decided tonight, halfway through our search, to give up, then we could always turn back, and it would be easy to make up a reasonable excuse for why our field trip had ended early.

(16) My family had bought the story that we were going on a field trip unquestioningly; all that we had to do was make sure that the school didn't call them when we didn't show up for classes on Friday. **(17)** Inès had faked a doctor's note that Sébastien would turn in, and I had made up a family vacation. **(18)** I seem to remember I said it was for President's Day, although in retrospect, I am shocked anyone would have believed that. **(19)** Whatever excuse I had made up, with little difficulty, we now had the whole day to ourselves. **(20)** We were free to do exactly what we wanted.

(21) It wouldn't have been hard for me to borrow a guidebook or city map for the excursion from my parents. **(22)** But obviously, knowing I would give up the whole plot if I asked them for anything like that, I had opted instead to just throw some water and snacks into my regular school satchel. **(23)** Inès, however, had showed up at the school gate that morning with a detailed plan and high-powered flashlights, and I felt like an amateur in contrast. **(24)** Despite all this, there was a *frisson* of excitement in the air as we set off underground—it was an early indication of what has developed into a somewhat reckless impulse in me to leave the map behind and explore freely.

1. The imagery of the first paragraph (sentences 1–6) primarily creates a feeling of

    Ⓐ mystery and tension

    Ⓑ openness and sense of comfort

    Ⓒ sadness and a hope for understanding

    Ⓓ suspense and fear

Passage

   To be precise, a moat is a deep, broad ditch dug around the outside of a fortification. It forms a perimeter and is designed as a first line of defense against attackers. The word "moat" came to Middle English from the Old French *motte*, meaning "mound." Originally, the word referred to the central island on which a fortress was built, but it eventually came to refer to the surrounding ring, suggesting a close relation between these two features in construction.

2. The author includes and defines the word *"motte"* primarily to

    Ⓐ offer a physical description of moats

    Ⓑ relate the name and origin of moats

    Ⓒ pinpoint the geographical source of moats

    Ⓓ indicate the military and protective value of moats

Passage

   At the onset of World War II, when the company Bausch & Lomb came up with a sunglass design for US Air Force pilots that would reduce glare—the sunglasses "banned" distracting rays to improve visibility—it immediately put all of its manufacturing resources into these Ray-Ban Aviators. Following the war, Americans sought the brand's "heroic" sunglasses, wanting to adopt the look of soldiers and aviators pictured in news photographs.

3. Why does the author place quotation marks around the word "heroic" (sentence 2)?

    Ⓐ To suggest that Ray-Ban Aviators, though part of a heroic cause, are not literally heroic

    Ⓑ To underscore how Ray-Ban Aviators aided US pilots

    Ⓒ To indicate that the US pilots used the word "heroic" to describe Ray-Ban Aviators

    Ⓓ To point out that the Ray-Ban company changed the sunglasses' name to include the word "heroic"

Wrap-Up

Instructions
Complete the wrap-up question. If time remains after you've finished, double-check your work.

Passage
Before World War I, the only timepieces created and sold for men were pocket watches—named for the fact that the watches were kept in the pocket—and wristwatches were worn exclusively by women as fashion accessories. During the war, pocket watches proved highly impractical for both soldiers in the trenches and aviators who needed to use both hands at all times, inspiring the development of men's wristwatches for civilian markets.

2. The author includes the information about women's fashion accessories primarily to

      (A) offer a physical description of wristwatches

      (B) indicate the convenience and value of wristwatches for soldiers

      (C) pinpoint the time period in which wristwatches were created

      (D) contrast the typical styles of watches worn during that time period

Synthesis: Central Arguments

In this chapter, you will evaluate the characteristics of TSIA2 synthesis questions that focus on the central arguments of two passages. In addition, you will review and apply a strategy that can be used to answer any TSIA2 question with those characteristics.

🎯 LEARNING TARGETS

1. Identify the characteristics of a synthesis question.

2. Compare the central arguments of two passages.

3. Utilize a prescribed strategy to eliminate incorrect answer choices.

 **Groundwork**

EXERCISE A

Instructions
Refer to the following question as your teacher leads the discussion. Do not answer the question.

Passage 1
Your learning style is not difficult to adapt to, and the average person can figure theirs out relatively easily. Whether you're a visual, auditory, or tactile learner, most teachers nowadays have the knowledge and resources to meet your needs. To discover your learning style, simply follow these essential steps. First, identify a particular method of learning and what that style entails. Second, list areas where you can put this type of learning into action. Third, commit to sticking to this method as firmly as possible (implementing visual learning might be easier with the help of a teacher). Fourth, and finally—compare with other methods! In a couple of months, you may have the educational breakthrough of a lifetime.

Passage 2
It's often thought that students learn best through one particular method of learning. That belief seems to have come from a study in the 1990s that found that teachers that reached the widest group of students used several instructional styles. However, approaching subject matter in various ways may be beneficial in and of itself, and the truth is people do not have only one style of learning. Indeed, a study in the *British Journal of Psychology* shows no correlation between reported learning style and memory. Of the 104 students in the experiment, one group reported preferring to remember pictures better than words. But the groups did not ultimately differ when put to the test.

1. The author of Passage 2 most likely would say that the argument expressed in Passage 1 is

   Ⓐ vague and dangerous

   Ⓑ researched and logical

   Ⓒ undeveloped but encouraging

   Ⓓ common but misguided

EXERCISE B

Instructions

Review the basic steps for answering a short passage question. Put them into the correct sequence by filling in numbers 1–5 in the space provided.

_____ Identify and compare the central argument of each passage.

_____ Read the question first.

_____ Read the passages.

_____ Find your evidence.

_____ Use the process of elimination.

Application

✓ THE APPROACH

When a synthesis question asks you about the central arguments of both passages, use these steps ...

1. Read the question.

2. Read the passages.

3. Identify and compare the central claim of each passage.

4. Find your evidence.

5. Use the process of elimination.

Passage 1

Your learning style is not difficult to adapt to, and the average person can figure theirs out relatively easily. Whether you're a visual, auditory, or tactile learner, most teachers nowadays have the knowledge and resources to meet your needs. To discover your learning style, simply follow these essential steps. First, identify a particular method of learning and what that style entails. Second, list areas where you can put this type of learning into action. Third, commit to sticking to this method as firmly as possible (implementing visual learning might be easier with the help of a teacher). Fourth, and finally—compare with other methods! In a couple of months, you may have the educational breakthrough of a lifetime.

Passage 2

It's often thought that students learn best through one particular method of learning. That belief seems to have come from a study in the 1990s that found that teachers that reached the widest group of students used several instructional styles. However, approaching subject matter in various ways may be beneficial in and of itself, and the truth is people do not have only one style of learning. Indeed, a study in the *British Journal of Psychology* shows no correlation between reported learning style and memory. Of the 104 students in the experiment, one group reported preferring to remember pictures better than words. But the groups did not ultimately differ when put to the test.

1. The author of Passage 2 most likely would say that the argument expressed in Passage 1 is

Ⓐ vague and dangerous

Ⓑ researched and logical

Ⓒ undeveloped but encouraging

Ⓓ common but misguided

⊘ THE APPROACH

When a synthesis question asks you about the central arguments of both passages, use these steps ...

1. Read the question.
2. Read the passages.
3. Identify and compare the central claim of each passage.
4. Find your evidence.
5. Use the process of elimination.

Passage 1

The use of online pseudonyms, or fake names, has been a point of controversy since the advent of the Internet. Pseudonyms provide users with privacy and anonymity, but this anonymity can embolden users to act irresponsibly because they know their actions carry no real-world consequences. As a result, pseudonymous users are more likely to harass others and post hateful comments. Additionally, pseudonyms can facilitate dangerous—or even criminal—online activities, such as scams in which a user pretends to be an authority figure and threatens people for money. Given these concerns, some social media platforms like Weibo and Facebook require users to post under their real names. These platforms also make efforts to link people's online and offline social networks to ensure that users are held accountable for their online behavior.

Passage 2

Anyone who reads comments on YouTube videos or news articles knows that anonymous users can post some vile stuff, presumably because they know it can't be tracked back to them. However, psychologists who study online anonymity argue that the platform should be held partially responsible for this behavior. In the "deindividuated" model of anonymity, people who feel anonymous start to lose their sense of individual identity. Without a strong personal identity, people rely on group identities and become much more susceptible to group influences. That's why people get caught up in destructive mobs in real life—and why they feel it's appropriate to imitate others who post hurtful comments online. But when a community firmly enforces positivity and prosocial norms, anonymous users are susceptible to those good influences too! Online platforms ought to invest more time into fostering positive communities so they can reap the benefits of anonymity.

2. Both authors would most likely agree with which statement?

  Ⓐ Pseudonyms are worth the risk because they provide much-needed privacy to users.

  Ⓑ Anonymity is inherently negative in both online and offline contexts.

  Ⓒ Online platforms can help to address the problems associated with anonymity.

  Ⓓ Using real names online is generally preferable, except in cases where group norms are well-enforced.

 **Practice**

Instructions

Complete the practice set. If time remains after you've finished, double-check your work.

Passage 1

Should time-consuming athletic programs be cut from schools? Ongoing research indicates the opposite. One study looked at various factors indicating the health and social values of both student athletes and their non-sport-playing peers. Researchers found that young people who play competitive sports tend to have a higher GPA and spend more hours studying than students who don't play sports. Additionally, rates of depression and anxiety are lower for student athletes than for their counterparts who don't play sports. Researchers also learned that student athletes are more likely to have an active, healthy lifestyle as they grow older than those who did not participate in sports. Already familiar with exercising, goal setting, and pushing through challenges, teen athletes can carry these habits into adulthood.

Passage 2

Playing defense on my high school's soccer team, I admit it's hard to focus on whatever is going on in class when it's game day. Practice days can be pretty grueling—we spend hours either in exhausting drills or in mandatory study hall to keep our GPA up. Before I played sports, I got more rest, and I had friends from different organizations around school. I knew other students because we rode the bus together or were in the same group for a science project. Now, I spend most of my time at practice, and since my teammates are my friends, it's natural to spend our free time together, too. Then again, what's free time?

1. The authors of both passages would probably characterize student athletes as being generally

Ⓐ overwhelmed

Ⓑ healthy

Ⓒ friendless

Ⓓ satisfied

Passage 1

As secondary education options become more diverse, liberal arts colleges are gaining popularity. The size of liberal arts colleges usually allows the students to be well acquainted with one another. Smaller class sizes also mean professors often have more one-on-one time with students. However, the cost of attendance may not be worth it, depending on what kind of lifestyle students expect to have in the future. Another option might be taking liberal arts classes at a state university rather than attending a private liberal arts school. This way, students can still receive a well-rounded education while avoiding many years of paying off student loans.

Passage 2

Many students today are choosing to go to a state university because of the greater number of opportunities available. Despite their "small classroom" advantages, private liberal arts schools can miss out on important government funding, so their facilities and resources can be lacking. Students may pay a higher tuition cost, spend more in student fees, and encounter higher prices in the cafeteria or recreation center. Ensuring job security after graduation is also crucial, and students are increasingly opting for majors that are perceived to lead more directly to jobs. A liberal arts college experience can be rewarding, but for many high school graduates, the high cost of tuition is not worth it.

2. Both authors would probably agree that for some students, going to a liberal arts college is

Ⓐ essential

Ⓑ unaffordable

Ⓒ practical

Ⓓ unfulfilling

This page is intentionally left blank.
Content resumes on the next page.

8

Synthesis: Evaluating Claims

In this chapter, you will evaluate the characteristics of a TSIA2 synthesis question that focuses on a single claim made within the larger context of the argument. In addition, you will review and apply a strategy that can be used to answer any TSIA2 question with those characteristics.

🎯 LEARNING TARGETS

1. Review the characteristics of a synthesis question.

2. Determine how an author would respond to the claim of an opposing argument.

3. Utilize a prescribed strategy to eliminate incorrect answer choices.

Groundwork

EXERCISE A

Instructions
Refer to the following question as your teacher leads the discussion. Do not answer the question.

Passage 1
A rising number of people are opting to work alone. In the United States, over one-fifth of the workforce describe themselves as "independent workers," and around the world, the number of people who typically work in a solitary setting is increasing as gig work becomes more prevalent. In a recent analysis, many independent workers reported not feeling lonely at work; in fact, the analysis indicates that people who are working alone spend more time making connections and attending networking events. It's possible that these workers appreciate that they can spend time collaborating with others and then return to a private office or turn off emails when they need uninterrupted work time. In more ways than one, it's having your cake and eating it too: coworking when you need it, but flexibility and independence whenever you want.

Passage 2
"Coworking" is an arrangement where professionals from different companies share a workspace and split costs such as rent and janitorial services, as well as enjoy office perks such as coffee, office supplies, and camaraderie. There are ever-growing numbers of coworking spaces across the US, such as community-run spaces that are open to the public, private offices that require a monthly or yearly subscription, and industry-specific spaces such as sites that cater to nonprofit sector employees. As the American workforce becomes gig economy-oriented and more people recognize the intrinsic loneliness of independent working, shared workspaces may play a larger role in our careers very soon.

1. The author of Passage 1 would probably respond to the reference in Passage 2 to the "intrinsic loneliness of independent working" by

   (A) pointing to the findings of the analysis described in Passage 1
   (B) casting doubt on the benefits of coworking mentioned in Passage 2
   (C) underscoring the notion that working alongside others makes people happier
   (D) emphasizing the pitfalls of working alone

EXERCISE B

Instructions

Review the basic steps for answering a synthesis question. Put them into the correct sequence by filling in numbers 1–5 in the space provided.

_____ Read the question first.

_____ Use the process of elimination.

_____ Find your evidence.

_____ Locate and review the details.

_____ Read the opposing author's passage.

Application

⊘ THE APPROACH

When a synthesis question asks you to evaluate a detail in one passage from the opposing author's perspective, use these steps …

1. Read the question first.
2. Locate and review the details.
3. Read the opposing author's passage.
4. Find your evidence.
5. Use the process of elimination.

Passage 1

A rising number of people are opting to work alone. In the United States, over one-fifth of the workforce describe themselves as "independent workers," and around the world, the number of people who typically work in a solitary setting is increasing as gig work becomes more prevalent. In a recent analysis, many independent workers reported not feeling lonely at work; in fact, the analysis indicates that people who are working alone spend more time making connections and attending networking events. It's possible that these workers appreciate that they can spend time collaborating with others and then return to a private office or turn off emails when they need uninterrupted work time. In more ways than one, it's having your cake and eating it too: coworking when you need it, but flexibility and independence whenever you want.

Passage 2

"Coworking" is an arrangement where professionals from different companies share a workspace and split costs such as rent and janitorial services, as well as enjoy office perks such as coffee, office supplies, and camaraderie. There are ever-growing numbers of coworking spaces across the US, such as community-run spaces that are open to the public, private offices that require a monthly or yearly subscription, and industry-specific spaces such as sites that cater to nonprofit sector employees. As the American workforce becomes gig economy-oriented and more people recognize the intrinsic loneliness of independent working, shared workspaces may play a larger role in our careers very soon.

1. The author of Passage 1 would probably respond to the reference in Passage 2 to the "intrinsic loneliness of independent working" by

   Ⓐ pointing to the findings of the analysis described in Passage 1

   Ⓑ casting doubt on the benefits of coworking mentioned in Passage 2

   Ⓒ underscoring the notion that working alongside others makes people happier

   Ⓓ emphasizing the pitfalls of working alone

⊘ THE APPROACH

When a synthesis question asks you to evaluate a detail in one passage from the opposing author's perspective, use these steps …

1. Read the question first.
2. Locate and review the details.
3. Read the opposing author's passage.
4. Find your evidence.
5. Use the process of elimination.

Passage 1

I recently met a ninth-grade teacher who told me that over half of her students drank coffee in the mornings. Some of her students said they started drinking coffee as early as sixth grade. Others said they only started in high school—where the gym vending machine sells cold coffee drinks. A handful of the non-coffee drinkers admitted they drink caffeinated soda to wake up every morning. As a matter of fact, about 64% of Americans have a cup of coffee every morning rather than waking up naturally. This is a shame! Now more than ever, people need to return to more natural ways of living—especially young, developing children. Parents, end your children's caffeine consumption and ensure they get enough sleep every night instead!

Passage 2

There are almost no conclusive statistics about the number of young people consuming caffeine daily. Fatigued students struggle to focus in class and perform poorly on tests, however, and many other nations with a culture of tea-drinking consistently have higher-scoring students than the United States. It's possible that American students are not as alert and productive as their caffeinated counterparts. Coffee and tea also contain antioxidants and some essential nutrients, so caffeinated drinks can provide a variety of benefits, from improved physical health to mental stimulation and clarity. In addition to encouraging a good night's sleep, it is logical for parents to allow their children to consume caffeine, including coffee, in the morning for their well-being.

2. The author of Passage 2 would probably respond to the last sentence of Passage 1 by

    Ⓐ arguing that children should be drinking more coffee in the mornings

    Ⓑ pointing out that children consume more caffeine at a young age than their parents did

    Ⓒ asserting that children should use more natural methods to wake up

    Ⓓ emphasizing that parents should help children balance rest and caffeine consumption

 Practice

Instructions

Complete the practice set. If time remains after you've finished, double-check your work.

Passage 1

Should time-consuming athletic programs be cut from schools? Ongoing research indicates the opposite. One study looked at various factors indicating the health and social values of both student athletes and their non–sport-playing peers. Researchers found that young people who play competitive sports tend to have a higher GPA and spend more hours studying than students who don't play sports. Additionally, rates of depression and anxiety are lower for student athletes than for their counterparts who don't play sports. Researchers also learned that student athletes are more likely to have an active, healthy lifestyle as they grow older than those who did not participate in sports. Already familiar with exercising, goal setting, and pushing through challenges, teen athletes can carry these habits into adulthood.

Passage 2

Playing defense on my high school's soccer team, I admit it's hard to focus on whatever is going on in class when it's game day. Practice days can be pretty grueling—we spend hours either in exhausting drills or in mandatory study hall to keep our GPA up. Before I played sports, I got more rest, and I had friends from different organizations around school. I knew other students because we rode the bus together or were in the same group for a science project. Now, I spend most of my time at practice, and since my teammates are my friends, it's natural to spend our free time together, too. Then again, what's free time?

1. What would the author of Passage 2 most likely say is the cause of the "more hours" (sentence 4) student athletes spend studying as mentioned in Passage 1?

   (A) the injuries caused by accidents during practice

   (B) the difficulty of completing homework with limited free time

   (C) the interruption to class due to traveling to away games

   (D) the requirement to maintain a high GPA

Passage 1

As secondary education options become more diverse, liberal arts colleges are gaining popularity. The size of liberal arts colleges usually allows the students to be well acquainted with one another. Smaller class sizes also mean professors often have more one-on-one time with students. However, the cost of attendance may not be worth it, depending on what kind of lifestyle students expect to have in the future. Another option might be taking liberal arts classes at a state university rather than attending a private liberal arts school. This way, students can still receive a well-rounded education while avoiding many years of paying off student loans.

Passage 2

Many students today are choosing to go to a state university because of the greater number of opportunities available. Despite their "small classroom" advantages, private liberal arts schools can miss out on important government funding, so their facilities and resources can be lacking. Students might pay a higher tuition cost, spend more in student fees, and encounter higher prices in the cafeteria or recreation center. Ensuring job security after graduation is also crucial, and studies have shown that students are increasingly avoiding the liberal arts and instead opting for majors that are perceived to lead more directly to jobs. A liberal arts college experience can be rewarding, but for many high school graduates, the high cost of tuition is not worth it.

2. The author of Passage 2 would most likely respond to the first sentence of Passage 1 ("As secondary . . . popularity") by

   (A) pointing to evidence that liberal arts programs are actually becoming less popular

   (B) requesting additional testimonials regarding the popularity of liberal arts programs

   (C) explaining that liberal arts programs are not the only ones gaining popularity

   (D) maintaining that the popularity of liberal arts programs is indeed increasing

This page is intentionally left blank.
Content resumes on the next page.

9

Short Passages

In this chapter, you will evaluate the characteristics of a short passage question from the TSIA2. In addition, you will review and apply a strategy that can be used to answer any TSIA2 question with those characteristics.

🎯 **LEARNING TARGETS**

1. Identify the characteristics of a short passage question.

2. Locate evidence within an informational text.

3. Utilize a prescribed strategy to eliminate incorrect answer choices.

Groundwork

EXERCISE A

Instructions
Refer to the following question as your teacher leads the discussion. Do not answer the question.

Passage

In 2012, volunteers for "Let's Do It! World," a worldwide movement to combat the global solid waste problem, planned a six-month series of cleanups around the globe. These "cleanup days" occurred in 96 different countries, including Estonia, Lebanon, Nepal, and the Philippines. Slovenia's cleanup day was the largest that year, with over 289,000 participants. The tradition is gaining momentum, and on February 9, 2014, country cleanup leaders from around the world agreed to the goal of involving 380 million people by 2018.

1. The passage suggests that the main goal of the cleanup days was to encourage people to

   (A) spend more time in nature

   (B) volunteer for meaningful causes

   (C) commit to making a cleaner planet

   (D) travel to neighboring countries

EXERCISE B

Instructions
Review the basic steps for answering a short passage question. Put them into the correct sequence by filling in numbers 1–4 in the space provided.

_____ Read the passage.

_____ Find your evidence.

_____ Use the process of elimination.

_____ Read the question first.

Application

✓ THE APPROACH

When answering a short passage question on the TSIA2, use these steps ...

1. Read the question first.
2. Read the passage.
3. Find your evidence.
4. Use the process of elimination.

Passage

In 2012, volunteers for "Let's Do It! World," a worldwide movement to combat the global solid waste problem, planned a six-month series of cleanups around the globe. These "cleanup days" occurred in 96 different countries, including Estonia, Lebanon, Nepal, and the Philippines. Slovenia's cleanup day was the largest that year, with over 289,000 participants. The tradition is gaining momentum, and on February 9, 2014, country cleanup leaders from around the world agreed to the goal of involving 380 million people by 2018.

1. The passage suggests that the main goal of the cleanup days was to encourage people to

   Ⓐ spend more time in nature

   Ⓑ volunteer for meaningful causes

   Ⓒ commit to making a cleaner planet

   Ⓓ travel to neighboring countries

⊘ THE APPROACH

When answering a short passage question on the TSIA2, use these steps ...

1. Read the question first.
2. Read the passage.
3. Find your evidence.
4. Use the process of elimination.

Passage

The red oak, the black oak, and the scarlet oak—all splendid forest trees of the Northeast—are so similar in appearance that they can often only be readily identified by the timber-cruiser, who knows every tree in the forest for its economic value, or by the botanist, with her paperback *Gray's Manual* in hand. I confess to bewilderment in five minutes after the differences have been explained to me, and I enjoyed, not long ago, the confusion of a skillful nurseryman who was endeavoring to show me his young trees of red oak that the label proved to be scarlet!

2. Which of the following best describes what "timber-cruiser" means, as it is used in the passage?

   Ⓐ a casual lover of nature who uses a guidebook for reference

   Ⓑ a botanist or scientist who has extensive knowledge of trees

   Ⓒ an individual who assesses the worth of trees for profit

   Ⓓ a nurseryman who must assign names to and label young trees

Practice

Instructions
Complete the practice set. If time remains after you've finished, double-check your work.

Passage
   When we think of blushing, embarrassment, redness, and a rise in temperature come to mind—all noticeable in the face. Most people are surprised to discover the phenomenon of blushing also occurs in the stomach. Because adrenaline causes tiny blood vessels called capillaries to widen and increase blood flow, the tissue around these vessels in the stomach appears as red as a blushing cheek. Though this may seem unnatural to some, the stomach is just another example of how the brain uses chemical processes to prepare the body for fight or flight in often unnoticed ways.

1. The main idea of the passage is that

   (A) blushing in the face is identical to blushing in the stomach

   (B) adrenaline causes blood vessels to widen for increased blood flow

   (C) the stomach is the most prepared part of the body for fight or flight

   (D) stomach blushing goes unnoticed but is a natural process

Passage
   A principal reason for the decline of opera singing in modern times is that the tuning of pitch has gradually and considerably risen during the last 150 years. As orchestras increasingly tune at higher frequencies, the vocal apparatus has been unable to bear the strain to which it is now subjected. With regard to tenors, though, the greater evil is that they disregard the falsetto register, singing everything, however high, in chest voice. Certainly they have not been beguiled into this serious mistake by the faint rise of tuning pitch just mentioned. The truth is that they have committed this fatal blunder knowingly and willfully—because they saw that it was more exciting to the public and knew it would draw in larger audiences.

2. Based on the passage, the rise of tuning pitch in music occurred

   (A) only in modern times

   (B) mainly due to the falsetto register

   (C) in the past two centuries

   (D) with the invention of a new apparatus

Passage

A narcissist is someone with obsessive admiration for the self and who shows a need for excessive attention or praise. The name comes from a tale in Greek mythology in which Narcissus, a hunter known for his beauty, became so attracted to his reflection in a pool of water that he fell in love. However, when the object of his affection could not love him back, Narcissus became distraught and withered away, leaving behind a narcissus flower.

3. What is the overall purpose of the passage?

    Ⓐ To recount a tale from Greek mythology

    Ⓑ To describe the origin of a word

    Ⓒ To stress the need to be cautious in love

    Ⓓ To demonstrate the difficulties of finding love

This page is intentionally left blank.
Content resumes on the next page.

Supporting Details

In this chapter, you will analyze a given text and answer questions by picking out details that explicitly support the requested information.

🎯 LEARNING TARGETS

1. Evaluate a question to target specific details.

2. Find relevant supporting details in the text.

3. Eliminate answers not supported by explicit information in the text.

Warm-Up

Instructions
Complete the warm-up question. If time remains after you've finished, double-check your work.

Passage

(1) That name, *Catacombes de Paris*. (2) It could mean more than a subterranean network of tunnels. (3) It could also refer to the complex interrelationships of the city itself: the crossroads of Paris. (4) There's adventure in that name, and mystery. (5) It's an intersection, a bridge to the afterlife, a place just underfoot. (6) The air felt as heavy with secrecy as it was with the smell of earth, with whispers, with mold.

(7) There were other memorable names to be found within the tunnels themselves: the *Sarcophagus of Lacrymatoire*, the *Fountain of the Samaritan*, their titles evocative of antiquity and myth, located in the bowels of the tunnels. (8) Looky-loos laden with cameras around their necks and guidebooks in hand hustled through the entrance, eager to make their own finds. (9) They talked loudly about the hidden treasures they expected to encounter as if their confidence might actually help locate them. (10) *The Sepulchral Lamp.* (11) *The Atelier.* (12) *The Crypt of Sacellum.*

(13) Inès had left to buy tickets. (14) I waited patiently by the entrance, scarcely believing that we were really going through with this but not quite nervous. (15) If we decided tonight, halfway through our search, to give up, then we could always turn back, and it would be easy to make up a reasonable excuse for why our field trip had ended early.

(16) My family had bought the story that we were going on a field trip unquestioningly; all that we had to do was make sure that the school didn't call them when we didn't show up for classes on Friday. (17) Inès had faked a doctor's note that Sébastien would turn in, and I had made up a family vacation. (18) I seem to remember I said it was for President's Day, although in retrospect I am shocked anyone would have believed that. (19) Whatever excuse I had made up, with little difficulty, we now had the whole day to ourselves. (20) We were free to do exactly what we wanted.

(21) It wouldn't have been hard for me to borrow a guidebook or city map for the excursion from my parents. (22) But obviously, knowing I would give up the whole plot if I asked them for anything like that, I had opted instead to just throw some water and snacks into my regular school satchel. (23) Inès, however, showed up at the school gate that morning with a detailed plan and high-powered flashlights, and I felt like an amateur in contrast. (24) Despite all this, there was a frisson of excitement in the air as we set off underground—it was an early indication of what has developed into a somewhat reckless impulse in me to leave the map behind and explore freely.

1. The primary setting of the passage is

    Ⓐ a school

    Ⓑ a museum

    Ⓒ a temple

    Ⓓ a burial site

Groundwork

EXERCISE A

Instructions

Use the following application to answer the questions below. Write your answers in the spaces provided.

NEW SERVER APPLICATION

Name: _____Margot Lowry_____

Age: ___19_____

Email: ___mlowry@applications.com_____

Phone: ___(209) 555-8392_____

Education:

    Thames High School

    Class of 2019

    Graduated top 10% in class

Experience:

    Babysitting — The Green Family

       • Cared for 3 small children, between the ages of 3 and 7

       • Prepared meals

       • Planned activities and crafts

       • Integrated learning into playtime activities

---

1. How old is Margot? _____

2. What family did Margot work for? _____

3. How did Margot improve playtime? _____

EXERCISE B

Instructions
Use the following passage to answer the questions below. Write your answers in the spaces provided.

Passage
(1) Wilbur and Orville dreamed of flight from the time they received their first toy rubber band helicopter from their father, Milton Wright, and they spent most of their lives building up the skills, funds, and research to make that dream a reality. (2) After dropping out of high school, Orville designed and built a printing press with Wilbur's help, and the two brothers opened up a print shop in their home of Dayton, Ohio, in 1889. (3) In 1892, the brothers moved into the bicycle business, starting a successful sales and repair shop in Dayton and later manufacturing their own brand of bicycle, also developed by Wright ingenuity.

4. Where did the Orville brothers spend their early adulthood?

    _____

5. After working in a print shop, the brothers opened what kind of business?

    _____

Application

✓ THE APPROACH

When answering a question that requires specific details from a text, use the following steps ...

1. Identify key words in the question.
2. Scan the passage for related key words.
3. Find your evidence near the key words.
4. Eliminate answer choices not directly supported by evidence.

Passage

The narrator of this passage, Nick Carraway, explains a bit about his background and family as he opens the story. Though he is not the main character of The Great Gatsby, *he provides the perspective through which the story is told.*

(1) My family have been prominent, well-to-do people in this Middle Western city for three generations. **(2)** The Carraways are something of a clan, and we have a tradition that we're descended from the Dukes of Buccleuch, but the actual founder of my line was my grandfather's brother, who came here in fifty-one, sent a substitute to the Civil War, and started the wholesale hardware business that my father carries on today.

(3) I never saw this great-uncle, but I'm supposed to look like him—with special reference to the rather hard-boiled painting that hangs in father's office. **(4)** I graduated from New Haven in 1915, just a quarter of a century after my father, and a little later I participated in that delayed Teutonic migration known as the Great War. **(5)** I enjoyed the counter-raid so thoroughly that I came back restless. **(6)** Instead of being the warm centre of the world, the Middle West now seemed like the ragged edge of the universe—so I decided to go East and learn the bond business. **(7)** Everybody I knew was in the bond business, so I supposed it could support one more single man. **(8)** All my aunts and uncles talked it over as if they were choosing a prep school for me, and finally said, "Why—ye-es," with very grave, hesitant faces. **(9)** Father agreed to finance me for a year, and after various delays I came East, permanently, I thought, in the spring of twenty-two.

From F. Scott Fitzgerald, *The Great Gatsby*

6. How did the narrator's family make its money?

Ⓐ in the bond business

Ⓑ through an inheritance from the Duke of Buccleuch

Ⓒ in the wholesale hardware business

Ⓓ by manufacturing and selling ammunition during the Civil War

Chapter 10: Supporting Details

TSIA2 Mastery: ELAR

⊘ THE APPROACH

When answering a question that requires specific details from a text, use the following steps ...

1. Identify key words in the question.
2. Scan the passage for related key words.
3. Find your evidence near the key words.
4. Eliminate answer choices not directly supported by evidence.

Passage

Many who were alive on November 22, 1963, remember the day that President John F. Kennedy, Jr. was assassinated while participating in a motorcade in Dallas, Texas, sending the world into a state of shock and grief. Incidentally, on the same date, two significant figures of literature, C.S. Lewis and Anthony Burgess, also passed away peacefully in their homes. Their deaths were as not as newsworthy, but they are still remembered for the bodies of work they left behind.

7. According to the passage, why did the deaths of Anthony Burgess and C. S. Lewis receive little news coverage?

   Ⓐ They were not important figures like President Kennedy.

   Ⓑ Because their work was not well-known, few people recognized their names.

   Ⓒ Their deaths coincided with the death of another extremely well-known figure.

   Ⓓ Their deaths were not reported by the local news outlets where they lived.

 **Practice**

Instructions

Complete the practice set. If time remains after you've finished, double-check your work.

Passage

This passage is from a short story in which the narrator describes her time in a Pennsylvania lakeside town.

(1) The time had come to bid fare-well to all my Morris Harbor friends, and my cozy room at the little inn, and return to the city that I worried would no longer be familiar. **(2)** There may be limits to such a winter's enjoyment, but the calm that accompanies a modest way of life is enticing enough to make up for the lack of finer pleasures, and the rewards of contentment are not for the restless.

(3) I was to travel the meandering local railway train that departed late in the day, and I sat for some time on the back porch overlooking the frozen blue lake, with loneliness as my companion. **(4)** Mrs. Cole had busied herself all day with tasks that seemingly required all of her attention; it was as if we were strangers passing one another in the street. **(5)** It was difficult to face my going-away with anything resembling a calm demeanor. **(6)** Finally I heard someone coming out onto the porch, and turned to see that Mrs. Cole was standing beside me.

(7) "Everything has been seen to," she announced suddenly with an unnaturally formal tone. **(8)** "Your cases must be down at the station by now. **(9)** The station-master he come an' carried 'em over himself, an' he'll make sure they're stowed in the luggage car. **(10)** Yes, I've seen to all your prep'rations," she said in a more familiar voice. **(11)** "The things I've put by the front door you'll want to keep with you; the sandwiches will do for your supper. **(12)** I suppose I shall walk down the Front Road now an' ask how old Mis' Robert Elwood is."

(13) I looked at my friend's face, and saw an expression that moved me deeply. **(14)** My emotions at leaving this place had already overwhelmed me.

(15) "I suppose you'll understand if I ain't over there to wave from the platform and see you off," she said, with her voice still brusque. **(16)** "Yes, I ought to find out how Mis' Robert Elwood is feelin'; if Mother comes on Tuesday she'll be askin' me how the old aunty is." **(17)** With this explanation, Mrs. Cole abruptly went back inside the inn, as if she had heard someone calling her name, so that I expected her to return, until I heard the front door closing and her footsteps on the path. **(18)** I could not bear such a departure; I hurried around the inn shouting after her, but she looked down and waved without turning around at the sound of my anxious voice, and so I walked away onto the road.

From Alice Mayne Corbett, *The Land of the Silver Maples*. Originally published in 1890.

1. Based on the passage, about how long has the narrator been in the town of Morris Harbor?

   Ⓐ since childhood

   Ⓑ a year

   Ⓒ a winter

   Ⓓ a week

2. The passage indicates that Mrs. Cole has helped the narrator by

    (A) finding her a room at the inn

    (B) making arrangements for her departure

    (C) inviting her to Mis' Elwood's

    (D) providing directions to the train station

Passage

The Palace of Westminster in London has stood underneath the tower we know today as "Big Ben" for over 160 years, but "Big Ben" wasn't made the clock tower's official name until 1921. Before then, it was "St. Stephen's Tower." However, in the seventeenth century, more people would have called it "The Clock Tower," "The East Tower," or, in honor of its largest bell, "Big Ben."

3. The official name of the tower above the Palace of Westminster prior to 1921 was

    (A) Big Ben

    (B) The Clock Tower

    (C) St. Stephen's Tower

    (D) The East Tower

Wrap-Up

Instructions
Complete the wrap-up question. If time remains after you've finished, double-check your work.

Passage
(1) That name, *Catacombes de Paris*. **(2)** It could mean more than a subterranean network of tunnels. **(3)** It could also refer to the complex interrelationships of the city itself: the crossroads of Paris. **(4)** There's adventure in that name, and mystery. **(5)** It's an intersection, a bridge to the afterlife, a place just underfoot. **(6)** The air felt as heavy with secrecy as it was with the smell of earth, with whispers, with mold.

(7) There were other memorable names to be found within the tunnels themselves: the *Sarcophagus of Lacrymatoire*, the *Fountain of the Samaritan*, their titles evocative of antiquity and myth, located in the bowels of the tunnels. **(8)** Looky-loos laden with cameras around their necks and guidebooks in hand hustled through the entrance, eager to make their own finds. **(9)** They talked loudly about the hidden treasures they expected to encounter as if their confidence might actually help locate them. **(10)** *The Sepulchral Lamp.* **(11)** *The Atelier.* **(12)** *The Crypt of Sacellum.*

(13) Inès had left to buy tickets. **(14)** I waited patiently by the entrance, scarcely believing that we were really going through with this but not quite nervous. **(15)** If we decided tonight, halfway through our search, to give up, then we could always turn back, and it would be easy to make up a reasonable excuse for why our field trip had ended early.

(16) My family had bought the story that we were going on a field trip unquestioningly; all that we had to do was make sure that the school didn't call them when we didn't show up for classes on Friday. **(17)** Inès had faked a doctor's note that Sébastien would turn in, and I had made up a family vacation. **(18)** I seem to remember I said it was for President's Day, although in retrospect I am shocked anyone would have believed that. **(19)** Whatever excuse I had made up, with little difficulty, we now had the whole day to ourselves. **(20)** We were free to do exactly what we wanted.

(21) It wouldn't have been hard for me to borrow a guidebook or city map for the excursion from my parents. **(22)** But obviously, knowing I would give up the whole plot if I asked them for anything like that, I had opted instead to just throw some water and snacks into my regular school satchel. **(23)** Inès, however, showed up at the school gate that morning with a detailed plan and high-powered flashlights, and I felt like an amateur in contrast. **(24)** Despite all this, there was a frisson of excitement in the air as we set off underground—it was an early indication of what has developed into a somewhat reckless impulse in me to leave the map behind and explore freely.

2. All of the following are presented to adults as reasons for the girls' absence EXCEPT

     (A) a field trip

     (B) a family vacation

     (C) a visiting relative

     (D) an illness

This page is intentionally left blank.
Content resumes on the next page.

11

Inferences

In this chapter, you will review the steps for drawing inferences from literary and informational texts by combining critical thinking and evidence from the text.

 **Warm-Up**

Instructions
Complete the warm-up question. If time remains after you've finished, double-check your work.

Passage
The Japanese Pagoda—a historic symbol of peace and unity located in Washington, D.C.—was actually created overseas. In 1957, the mayor of Yokohama, Japan, gifted the sculpture to the city of Washington, D.C., as a sign of friendship following World War II. Constructed in Japan, the sculpture was broken down, packed into five crates, and delivered to Washington, D.C., as a puzzle without instructions for reassembly. It then took several weeks for Smithsonian specialists to reconstruct the sculpture.

1. Which of the following can be inferred from the passage?

   Ⓐ The United States and Japan continued fighting after World War II.

   Ⓑ The Japanese Pagoda was too big to be shipped to Washington, D.C., in one piece.

   Ⓒ The reconstruction of the Japanese Pagoda took longer than initially thought.

   Ⓓ The Japanese Pagoda is no longer the symbol of friendly diplomatic relations it once was.

Groundwork

EXERCISE A

Instructions
Use the passage and suspects' statements to figure out who filled the stadium with balloons.

Passage
When the football team at Central High School arrived at the stadium for practice at the end of the first day of school, they found that it had been completely filled with balloons. The coach had been in the stadium right before lunch, so he knew that it was filled between lunch and 3:30. After some investigation, the coach narrowed down the list of potential pranksters to 4 staff members. Each of them provided a statement as to their whereabouts when the prank was committed.

Suspect #1: The Maintenance Man

Statement: I was working on repairing a faulty air conditioning unit, so there's no way it could've been me.

Suspect #2: The Cheerleading Coach

Statement: I totally think the balloons were *brilliant,* especially since they were school colors, but it wasn't me. I spent all day decorating the cafeteria for the "Welcome Back!" dance.

Suspect #3: The Principal's Secretary

Statement: I was grocery shopping trying to make sure the concession stand would be stocked, so I wasn't even on campus at the time.

Suspect #4: The Math Teacher

Statement: Is it even possible to give a mid-term exam *and* fill the stadium with balloons at the same time? I think not. I was in my classroom the whole time, making sure students were keeping their eyes on their own papers.

EXERCISE B

Instructions
Read the passage. Then, determine if each statement is an accurate inference based on the evidence provided. Circle your answer.

Passage

Sherlock Holmes is best known for his amazing deductive skills. He can take a look at someone's hat and automatically know all kinds of details about that person, like where they've been or what they do for a living. Many of his adventures begin at 221B Baker Street, which is where he lives with his partner Dr. John Watson. Together, they help a variety of clients, including Scotland Yard, solve mysteries. Sir Arthur Conan Doyle may not have been the first author to develop a detective character for his story, but in creating Sherlock Holmes, he created the most celebrated of them all.

1. Sherlock Holmes is a fictional character.

        Supported   Not Enough Evidence

2. Without Sherlock Holmes, Scotland Yard would be unable to solve many cases.

        Supported   Not Enough Evidence

3. Holmes and Watson spend a lot of time together.

        Supported   Not Enough Evidence

EXERCISE C

Instructions
Read the passage. Then, determine which statements are supported by the passage. Circle any statements that make an accurate inference.

Passage
Nancy Drew is fashionable, brave, curious, and resourceful. And, she's completely fictional. However, that fact is dismissed when it comes to the millions who see her as an exceptional role model. In fact, her novels have remained in pop culture since 1930, which is more than most protagonists from children's stories can say. Along with her dog, Togo, Nancy spends her time devoted to unearthing the truth behind each and every mystery she encounters. Even more, the stories do not delve into controversial topics, such as religion or politics, providing a safe context for readers to escape from their daily lives and into an adrenaline-inducing adventure.

4. Nancy Drew was born in the 1930s.

5. Nancy's adventures often involved escaping from kidnappers.

6. The *Nancy Drew* series is considered children's fiction.

 **Application**

⊘ THE APPROACH

When a question asks you to make an inference based on a passage, use these steps …

1. Identify the topic of the question.
2. Find evidence in the passage.
3. Eliminate answers that are not supported by the evidence.

Passage

On December 9, 2019, about 100 adventure tourists and guides traveled to White Island, an active stratovolcano near New Zealand, for a chance to hike in the caldera, see a bubbling acidic lake, and experience the sensation of walking on another world. About half of the tourists had already departed the island when the volcano erupted, shooting a column of steam and ash a mile into the air, followed by a horizontal blast of super-heated gases and ash that covered the island in an instant. Rescue crews assembled and were ready to fly to the island, but they were sent to a different island due to strict governmental health and safety regulations that prevented them from entering an unsafe area. Initially, a police spokesperson explained that there were no signs of life on the island, but volunteer rescuers later removed 31 people from the island by boat and helicopter, saving the lives of 24 tourists.

7. Which of the following can be inferred from the passage?

   (A) The volunteer rescuers are braver than the first responders.

   (B) The volcanic gases in the atmosphere make it impossible for helicopters to fly to the island.

   (C) Governmental safety policies meant to protect the lives of first responders risked the lives of the victims.

   (D) Before the volcano erupted, rescue crews assembled and conducted an on-foot search for signs of life on the island.

✓ THE APPROACH

When a question asks you to make an inference based on a passage, use these steps …

1. Identify the topic of the question.
2. Find evidence in the passage.
3. Eliminate answers that are not supported by the evidence.

Passage

Adventure tourism isn't just for the most able-bodied and athletic of the human population anymore. These adrenaline-filled vacations are available for anyone, regardless of age, physical abilities, or intellectual limitations. Known as "accessible tourism," these opportunities provide the inclusive benefits that allow anyone who wishes to participate in a variety of thrilling activities. Through the use of newly-designed accessibility features, highly trained staff, and a modern perspective of zero tolerance for limitations, companies are paving the way for equitable access to some of life's greatest thrills.

8. Which of the following can be inferred from the passage?

Ⓐ Not everyone wants to spend their vacation on thrill-seeking activities.

Ⓑ Before accessible tourism, not everyone could participate in adventure tourism.

Ⓒ The adventure tourism industry is the most popular vacation option in the United States.

Ⓓ The industry's accessibility features are extremely costly.

Practice

Instructions

Complete the practice set. If time remains after you've finished, double-check your work.

Passage

While traveling around Seattle, Washington, to discover new bands in the Pacific Northwest, Jonathan Poneman of Sub Pop Records asked the unknown Kurt Cobain about a demo he had allegedly made. He adamantly denied its existence. However, as Poneman was leaving town, Cobain came to his hotel and handed him the demo saying, "Listen before I change my mind." What Poneman heard would launch one of the best-selling bands of all time, the pioneers of a 1990s music revolution: Nirvana.

1. The passage implies that Cobain's initial feeling about interest in his demo was

    Ⓐ unease

    Ⓑ indignation

    Ⓒ gratification

    Ⓓ enthusiasm

Passage

Marquees are often used to lure audiences to cinemas and theaters. The very first marquees were rather small and hardly protruded from the building's façade. In the early 20th century, these would display information to people walking by or entering the theater. It was not until the popularization of the automobile that marquees were made to be larger and to broadcast their messages boldly to attract people to shows.

2. We can infer that the reason the marquees were made larger was that

    Ⓐ the displays of the early 20th century were considered unsatisfactory

    Ⓑ smaller marquees display less information than larger ones

    Ⓒ it is hard to read smaller marquees while driving

    Ⓓ marquees that were part of building façades were not architecturally sound

Passage

Most bars are set up to allow patrons to open a "tab" and settle their bill in one transaction when ready to leave. However, many bars used to manage tabs much differently. Certain customers were permitted to settle their tab at the end of the week on their payday, allowing them to leave and never return (of course, this was hardly common because these tabs were only extended to regular customers). These patrons were sometimes called "trust customers" because the bartender trusts that they will pay fairly.

3. It can be inferred that bartenders welcomed "trust customers" in part because bar patrons

    Ⓐ are generally honorable

    Ⓑ hardly ever put purchases on tabs

    Ⓒ are wealthier than average

    Ⓓ typically are returning customers

 **Wrap-Up**

Instructions
Complete the wrap-up question. If time remains after you've finished, double-check your work.

Passage
During the process of anaerobic digestion, animal waste produces methane gas. Recently, biochemists sponsored by the Department of Energy discovered a way to make synthetic versions of waste that give off even more methane. You might be asking why the Department of Energy is sponsoring such developments. The reason is that methane produced by such waste could someday generate enough electricity for a whole city.

2. What assumption does the author of the passage make?

(A) Gases made from waste will be cheaper to make than other gases.

(B) The Department of Energy has already been using methane-generating waste for electricity.

(C) Synthetic algae will not be able to undergo anaerobic digestion.

(D) Readers would not typically link the Department of Energy with animal waste research.

Trap Answers

In this chapter, you will learn how to spot and avoid typical trap answers seen in the reading portion of the TSIA2 ELAR multiple-choice section.

Groundwork

Instructions

Review the instructions for a reading question from the TSIA2. Then, refer to the passage and question as your teacher leads the discussion. Do not answer the question.

Read the passage below and then choose the best answer to each question. Answer the questions on the basis of what is <u>stated</u> or <u>implied</u> in the passage.

Passage

(1) Six years have passed since I resolved on my present undertaking. **(2)** I can, even now, remember the hour from which I dedicated myself to this great enterprise. **(3)** I commenced by inuring my body to hardship. **(4)** I accompanied the whale-fishers on several expeditions to the North Sea; I voluntarily endured cold, famine, thirst, and want of sleep; I often worked harder than the common sailors during the day and devoted my nights to the study of mathematics, the theory of medicine, and those branches of physical science from which a naval adventurer might derive the greatest practical advantage. **(5)** Twice I actually hired myself as an under-mate in a Greenland whaler, and acquitted myself to admiration. **(6)** I must own I felt a little proud when my captain offered me the second dignity in the vessel and entreated me to remain with the greatest earnestness, so valuable did he consider my services.

(7) And now, dear Margaret, do I not deserve to accomplish some great purpose? **(8)** My life might have been passed in ease and luxury, but I preferred glory to every enticement that wealth placed in my path. **(9)** Oh, that some encouraging voice would answer in the affirmative! **(10)** My courage and my resolution is firm; but my hopes fluctuate, and my spirits are often depressed. **(11)** I am about to proceed on a long and difficult voyage, the emergencies of which will demand all my fortitude: I am required not only to raise the spirits of others, but sometimes to sustain my own, when theirs are failing.

(12) This is the most favourable period for travelling in Russia. **(13)** They fly quickly over the snow in their sledges; the motion is pleasant, and, in my opinion, far more agreeable than that of an English stagecoach. **(14)** The cold is not excessive, if you are wrapped in furs—a dress which I have already adopted, for there is a great difference between walking the deck and remaining seated motionless for hours, when no exercise prevents the blood from actually freezing in your veins. **(15)** I have no ambition to lose my life on the post-road between St. Petersburgh and Archangel.

From Mary Wollstonecraft Shelley, *Frankenstein; or, The Modern Prometheus*. Originally published in 1818.

1. According to the passage, the narrator wanted to experience the hardships mentioned in the first paragraph because

   (A) he had lost his fortune and needed to learn a skill to support himself.

   (B) the captain of a Greenland whaler ship asked him to provide his services.

   (C) he values the opinion of the captain more than anyone else.

   (D) he had spent most of his life living in leisure and privilege.

EXERCISE B

Instructions
Write the letter of each definition next to its matching term.

_____ Recycled Words

A. Presents information from the passage in an inaccurate way.

_____ Distractor

B. Offers details not mentioned in the passage.

_____ Outlier

C. Contains words from the passage within an incorrect statement.

Instructions

Review the statement made by a defendant in a court trial. Then, review the notes taken by three of the jury members. Determine which type of trap answer appears in each note and circle your answer.

Defendant's Statement

It had been a long day, and all I wanted was some chicken nuggets. I drove up to the speaker where you order, told them what I wanted, and waited in line. It took *forever* for them to serve the cars in front of me. There were only three of them! By the time I got to the window, I was so hungry I was about to take a bite out of my steering wheel. That's when everything broke down. I realized that I had forgotten my wallet at home, so I had no way to pay. I begged and pleaded for them to please just give me one nugget. One little nugget! They refused, and something in my brain snapped. It was at that point I launched a three-and-a-half-foot alligator through the window and sped away. After refusing my nugget request, I made sure karma would come back around and bite them.

Juror #1 – Notes

The alligator (named Karma) took a bite out of the steering wheel before being launched through the drive-through window.

Circle One: Recycled Words   Outlier   Distractor

Juror #2 – Notes

The defendant had planned to throw the alligator through the window the whole time.

Circle One: Recycled Words   Outlier   Distractor

Juror #3 – Notes

The defendant clearly isn't cut out for a job in customer service, but they could be a good candidate for a job at a reptile rehab facility.

Circle One: Recycled Words   Outlier   Distractor

Application

✓ THE APPROACH

When answering a reading question that requires finding exact information or making an inference based on a passage, use these steps ...

1. Read the question and passage.

2. Find your evidence.

3. Eliminate answer choices that are not supported by the passage.

Passage

(1) Six years have passed since I resolved on my present undertaking. (2) I can, even now, remember the hour from which I dedicated myself to this great enterprise. (3) I commenced by inuring my body to hardship. (4) I accompanied the whale-fishers on several expeditions to the North Sea; I voluntarily endured cold, famine, thirst, and want of sleep; I often worked harder than the common sailors during the day and devoted my nights to the study of mathematics, the theory of medicine, and those branches of physical science from which a naval adventurer might derive the greatest practical advantage. (5) Twice I actually hired myself as an under-mate in a Greenland whaler, and acquitted myself to admiration. (6) I must own I felt a little proud when my captain offered me the second dignity in the vessel and entreated me to remain with the greatest earnestness, so valuable did he consider my services.

(7) And now, dear Margaret, do I not deserve to accomplish some great purpose? (8) My life might have been passed in ease and luxury, but I preferred glory to every enticement that wealth placed in my path. (9) Oh, that some encouraging voice would answer in the affirmative! (10) My courage and my resolution is firm; but my hopes fluctuate, and my spirits are often depressed. (11) I am about to proceed on a long and difficult voyage, the emergencies of which will demand all my fortitude: I am required not only to raise the spirits of others, but sometimes to sustain my own, when theirs are failing.

(12) This is the most favourable period for travelling in Russia. (13) They fly quickly over the snow in their sledges; the motion is pleasant, and, in my opinion, far more agreeable than that of an English stagecoach. (14) The cold is not excessive, if you are wrapped in furs—a dress which I have already adopted, for there is a great difference between walking the deck and remaining seated motionless for hours, when no exercise prevents the blood from actually freezing in your veins. (15) I have no ambition to lose my life on the post-road between St. Petersburgh and Archangel.

From Mary Wollstonecraft Shelley, *Frankenstein; or, The Modern Prometheus*. Originally published in 1818.

TSIA2 Mastery: ELAR

Chapter 12: Trap Answers

1. According to the passage, the narrator wanted to experience the hardships mentioned in the first paragraph because

   Ⓐ he had lost his fortune and needed to learn a skill to support himself.

   Ⓑ the captain of a Greenland whaler ship asked him to provide his services.

   Ⓒ he values the opinion of the captain more than anyone else.

   Ⓓ he had spent most of his life living in leisure and privilege.

 **Practice**

Instructions

Complete the practice set. If time remains after you've finished, double-check your work.

Passage 1

Life is a highway, or so the song goes. One is free to drive wherever they please, but that doesn't mean that driving is free. Who should pay for roads? How should they be maintained? The most straightforward answer is a simple toll system that requires each person to pay a small fee when they use a road—say one dollar per use. Those who drive the most pay the most because they use the road more frequently, but that is reasonable. And when everyone who uses the road pays a small, equal fee each time, repairs are done faster and driver satisfaction increases.

Passage 2

A toll road system, while appealing in its simplicity, has nothing to do with equity. Let's suppose that each person who uses the road daily pays a total of fifty dollars each month. A person making $100,000 a year would spend less than 1% of their monthly income on tolls, while a person making $20,000 would pay 3% of their monthly income. The tolls would be equal for all who use the road, which might seem reasonable. But this "reasonable" idea does not hold when we look at the true impact on real people. It probably wouldn't be difficult for a higher earner to spend $600 a year on tolls, but for the lower earner, having to budget $50 each month would surely affect their finances on a daily basis. Same fee, substantially different burden.

1. The author of Passage 2 would likely find fault with the author of Passage 1 for

   (A) not proving that charging tolls for roads is reasonable and fair

   (B) neglecting to mention how collecting tolls would benefit local governments

   (C) distorting and exaggerating the ease of updating roads to include tolls

   (D) failing to acknowledge the effects of tolls on certain people

2. Passage 1 suggests that

   (A) highways that require tolls are superior to those that don't.

   (B) small, equal fees are easier to budget for than larger, less frequent ones.

   (C) tolls divide the financial burden of road upkeep among drivers fairly.

   (D) drivers are happier when they have shorter commutes.

3. Which of the following can be inferred from Passage 2?

   Ⓐ Toll roads are easier to plan and build than other kinds of roads.

   Ⓑ The practice of charging tolls is more common in some parts of the world.

   Ⓒ Roads that charge tolls are preferred by those who drive long distances frequently.

   Ⓓ Charging equal road tolls impacts some people more than others.

This page is intentionally left blank.
Content resumes on the next page.

Essay Revision

In this chapter, you will evaluate the characteristics of an essay revision question from the TSIA2. In addition, you will review and apply a strategy that can be used to answer any TSIA2 question with those characteristics.

🎯 LEARNING TARGETS

1. Identify the characteristics of an essay revision problem.

2. Differentiate between composition-focused and grammar-focused questions.

3. Utilize a prescribed strategy to eliminate incorrect answer choices.

 **Groundwork**

EXERCISE A

Instructions
Refer to the following question as your teacher leads the discussion. Do not answer the question.

Passage
(1) Technology could one day be driving your car. **(2)** It is more than just the power behind texting or video games. **(3)** According to the latest research, technology may soon replace human drivers in the form of self-driving cars.

(4) Up until recently, autopilots were common on planes or in agricultural harvesting, but the development of the self-driving car never saw significant progress. **(5)** One reason why self-driving cars have yet to take off as a modern commuting option is the fact that they must navigate intricate and complex roadways. **(6)** In contrast, the air, sea, and even the surface of Mars are far simpler, with no traffic lights or stray children to run into the path. **(7)** For years, autonomous submarines have roamed wide-open waters, and driverless trains have followed limited, straightforward tracks.

(8) A second reason for the delay in the development of self-driving cars is that they require specialized, up-to-date maps. **(9)** Modern technology is teeming with online maps and GPS programs. **(10)** However, for self-driving cars to be successful, GPS isn't sufficient; a reliable backup system is necessary. **(11)** "We are currently developing artificial intelligence that allows an automated car to navigate new roads without [the use of] 3D maps, using a series of sensors that observe road conditions," Leslie Sanchez, chief engineer at Plymouth Labs, said.

(12) New car models include features that take over driving if the car swerves out of its lane or if vehicles in front of it stop suddenly. **(13)** These are examples of self-driving technology. **(14)** They say self-driving cars will lower the frequency of accidents on the road and reduce traffic.

1. In context, which of the following sentences would best be inserted between sentences 9 and 10?

    (A) Recent developments indicate that driverless cars may also one day replace ambulance drivers responding to emergencies.

    (B) Developing backup technology will likely take another decade.

    (C) Garmin Ltd., for example, provides GPS and mapping for a variety of users.

    (D) Many think self-driving cars could one day replace taxis and buses.

EXERCISE B

Instructions
Review the basic steps for answering an essay revision question. Put them into the correct sequence by filling in numbers 1–4 in the space provided.

_____   Determine the question type.

_____   Read the passage.

_____   Use the process of elimination.

_____   Use the right strategy.

Application

✓ THE APPROACH

When answering an essay revision question on the TSIA2, use these steps ...

1. Read the passage.
2. Determine the question type.
3. Use the right strategy.
4. Use the process of elimination.

Passage

(1) Technology could one day be driving your car. (2) It is more than just the power behind texting or video games. (3) According to the latest research, technology may soon replace human drivers in the form of self-driving cars.

(4) Up until recently, autopilots were common on planes or in agricultural harvesting, but the development of the self-driving car never saw significant progress. (5) One reason why self-driving cars have yet to take off as a modern commuting option is the fact that they must navigate intricate and complex roadways. (6) In contrast, the air, sea, and even the surface of Mars are far simpler, with no traffic lights or stray children to run into the path. (7) For years, autonomous submarines have roamed wide-open waters, and driverless trains have followed limited, straightforward tracks.

(8) A second reason for the delay in the development of self-driving cars is that they require specialized, up-to-date maps. (9) Modern technology is teeming with online maps and GPS programs. (10) However, for self-driving cars to be successful, GPS isn't sufficient; a reliable backup system is necessary. (11) "We are currently developing artificial intelligence that allows an automated car to navigate new roads without [the use of] 3D maps, using a series of sensors that observe road conditions," Leslie Sanchez, chief engineer at Plymouth Labs, said.

(12) New car models include features that take over driving if the car swerves out of its lane or if vehicles in front of it stop suddenly. (13) These are examples of self-driving technology. (14) They say self-driving cars will lower the frequency of accidents on the road and reduce traffic.

1. In context, which of the following sentences would best be inserted between sentences 9 and 10?

    (A) Recent developments indicate that driverless cars may also one day replace ambulance drivers responding to emergencies.

    (B) Developing backup technology will likely take another decade.

    (C) Garmin Ltd., for example, provides GPS and mapping for a variety of users.

    (D) Many think self-driving cars could one day replace taxis and buses.

⊘ THE APPROACH

When answering an essay revision question on the TSIA2, use these steps ...

1. Read the passage.
2. Determine the question type.
3. Use the right strategy.
4. Use the process of elimination.

Passage

(1) Technology could one day be driving your car. (2) It is more than just the power behind texting or video games. (3) According to the latest research, technology may soon replace human drivers in the form of self-driving cars.

(4) Up until recently, autopilots were common on planes or in agricultural harvesting, but the development of the self-driving car never saw significant progress. (5) One reason why self-driving cars have yet to take off as a modern commuting option is the fact that they must navigate intricate and complex roadways. (6) In contrast, the air, sea, and even the surface of Mars are far simpler, with no traffic lights or stray children to run into the path. (7) For years, autonomous submarines have roamed wide-open waters, and driverless trains have followed limited, straightforward tracks.

(8) A second reason for the delay in the development of self-driving cars is that they require specialized, up-to-date maps. (9) Modern technology is teeming with online maps and GPS programs. (10) However, for self-driving cars to be successful, GPS isn't sufficient; a reliable backup system is necessary. (11) "We are currently developing artificial intelligence that allows an automated car to navigate new roads without [the use of] 3D maps, using a series of sensors that observe road conditions," Leslie Sanchez, chief engineer at Plymouth Labs, said.

(12) New car models include features that take over driving if the car swerves out of its lane or if vehicles in front of it stop suddenly. (13) These are examples of self-driving technology. (14) They say self-driving cars will lower the frequency of accidents on the road and reduce traffic.

2. In context, which is the best revision to sentence 14 (reproduced below)?

   They say self-driving cars will lower the frequency of accidents on the road and reduce traffic.

   Ⓐ Replace "They say" with "Developers argue."

   Ⓑ Replace "will lower" with "will reduce."

   Ⓒ Delete "and reduce traffic."

   Ⓓ Insert "their" before "accidents."

 **Practice**

Instructions
Complete the practice set. If time remains after you've finished, double-check your work.

Passage
(1) Why do some people enjoy being scared? **(2)** You might be someone who happily pays money for scary movies, haunted houses, or terrifying thrill rides. **(3)** There's actually a scientific explanation behind this affinity. **(4)** Social psychologist Dr. Clark McCauley of Bryn Mawr College explains it like this: "The fictional nature of horror films affords viewers a sense of control by placing psychological distance between them and the violent acts they have witnessed." **(5)** Dr. McCauley received his Ph.D. from the University of Pennsylvania.

(6) Research has shown that stressed or anxious viewers actually feel better after watching horror movies. **(7)** They ultimately help by allowing their brains to artificially focus on survival instead of the issues in their lives that were previously causing worry or fear. **(8)** When you're scared, your prefrontal cortex, responsible for planning and decision making, becomes overshadowed by the limbic system, which controls arousal and stimulation. **(9)** Coming down from this adrenaline rush gives anxious viewers a sense of calm when a movie finishes, so it is not uncommon for sufferers to seek thrills and scares for therapeutic purposes.

1. What is the best way to combine sentences 6 and 7 (reproduced below)?

    Research has shown that stressed or anxious viewers actually feel better after watching horror movies. They ultimately help by allowing their brains to artificially focus on survival instead of the issues in their lives that were previously causing worry or fear.

    (A) Research has shown that stressed or anxious viewers actually feel better after watching horror movies, they ultimately help by allowing their brains to artificially focus on survival instead of the issues in their lives that were previously causing worry or fear.

    (B) Research has shown that stressed or anxious viewers actually feel better after watching horror movies ultimately these movies help by allowing their brains to artificially focus on survival instead of the issues in their lives that were previously causing worry or fear.

    (C) Research has shown that stressed or anxious viewers actually feel better after watching horror movies, which ultimately help by allowing their brains to artificially focus on survival instead of the issues in their lives that were previously causing worry or fear.

    (D) Research has shown that stressed or anxious viewers actually feel better after watching horror movies; then, they ultimately help by allowing their brains to artificially focus on survival instead of the issues in their lives that were previously causing worry or fear.

2. Which of the following sentences contains irrelevant information that can be deleted from the passage?

    (A) Sentence 1

    (B) Sentence 3

    (C) Sentence 5

    (D) Sentence 8

3. Where in the second paragraph should the following sentence be inserted?

    These fears are temporarily calmed by the body.

    (A) After sentence 6

    (B) After sentence 7

    (C) After sentence 8

    (D) After sentence 9

This page is intentionally left blank.
Content resumes on the next page.

Concision

In this chapter, you will review the concepts of redundancy and wordiness. You will correct concision errors by removing unnecessary words and phrases.

🎯 LEARNING TARGETS

1. Recognize phrases that are repetitive or wordy in nature.

2. Revise sentences for concision.

3. Evaluate answer choices to determine whether necessary information was removed.

Warm-Up

Instructions

Complete the warm-up question. If time remains after you've finished, double-check your work.

Passage

(1) When schools of fish gather again after time apart, they will swim around each other while waving their fins and performing elaborate dances. **(2)** Stingrays have been seen frolicking over fields of coral, twirling and flapping their wings, even when ample open ocean is readily available. **(3)** Some have argued that these kinds of behaviors show that fish can feel emotions like joy and delight.

(4) Even advocates for the argument that fish have feelings acknowledge that scientists can easily misidentify what they are seeing with their eyes. **(5)** The shape of a fish's mouth makes it look like it is surprised; it looks that way even when it is excited or in danger. **(6)** Fish are social, communicating underwater using clicks and bubbles. **(7)** Feelings are challenging to understand even in humans, who have the ability to talk about their emotions.

(8) Many oceanographers who devote their time to studying fish behavior have argued that at least some fish, such as triggerfishes and eels, have strong feelings like the ones we experience as humans. **(9)** Other researchers are doubtful. **(10)** They argue that it has not yet been proven that fish feel emotion in any reliable, reproducible scientific experiments.

(11) Regardless, scientific consensus on the question of fish emotion is beginning to undergo a shift. **(12)** Many biologists have accepted that fish most likely have "primary" emotions such as fear or anger. **(13)** These responses seem to be found in most fish. **(14)** For instance, a zebrafish will avoid a part of the tank where it was once shocked even if the shock has been removed. **(15)** Additionally, scientists believe that feelings can be inferred from fishes' changes in activity and eye movement, or even from involuntary responses like scale shedding.

1. Which of the following is the best version of the underlined portion of sentence 1 (reproduced below)?

   When schools of fish gather <u>again after time apart,</u> they will swim around each other while waving their fins and performing elaborate dances.

   Ⓐ (as it is now)
   Ⓑ after they have had separation between them,
   Ⓒ again after they have not been near each other for a while,
   Ⓓ together after they haven't gotten together for a while,

Groundwork

EXERCISE A

Instructions
Underline the part of the sentence that could be replaced by an abbreviation. Then, select an abbreviation to replace what you underlined.

| ASAP | etc. | vs. |

1. The store sells gloves, shoes, belts, and many other similar types of leather-based things.

   Abbreviation: _____

2. Sometimes it feels like me on one side going up against everything else in the world.

   Abbreviation: _____

3. Please return the key as soon as you possibly and reasonably can.

   Abbreviation: _____

EXERCISE B

Instructions
Review the following sentences as your teacher leads the discussion.

4. I couldn't believe what I was hearing with my ears.

5. Sharing her point of view, Doctor Lee gave her perspective on the illness and wrote out a prescription for the patient.

6. The first performance of the recital, Dana's dance was the perfect number to open the beginning of the evening.

    Revised: _____

Application

⊘ THE APPROACH

When the answer choices offer different phrasings of the same information, use the following steps ...

1. Eliminate answers with redundant information.

2. Eliminate answers with wordy phrases.

3. Select the most concise answer that does not lose any important information.

---

7. Which of the following is the best version of the underlined portion of the sentence below?

    In industrialized countries, air pollution can stem from a number of many various, different, and simultaneous factors.

    Ⓐ (as it is now)

    Ⓑ from a number of many and various factors.

    Ⓒ from a lot of different factors happening at the same time.

    Ⓓ from a number of simultaneous factors.

✅ THE APPROACH

When the answer choices offer different phrasings of the same information, use the following steps ...

1. Eliminate answers with redundant information.
2. Eliminate answers with wordy phrases.
3. Select the most concise answer that does not lose any important information.

8. Which of the following is the best version of the underlined portion of the sentence below?

   Many of the people who play baseball in the major leagues hail from countries outside the United States, such as the Dominican Republic and Venezuela.

   Ⓐ (as it is now)
   Ⓑ Many of the baseball players
   Ⓒ Many major league baseball players
   Ⓓ Many of the players who participate in the major leagues of baseball

 **Practice**

Instructions

Complete the practice set. If time remains after you've finished, double-check your work.

1. Which of the following is the best version of the underlined portion of the sentence below?

   Many oceanographers who devote their time to studying fish behavior have argued that at least some fish, such as triggerfishes and eels, <u>have strong feelings</u> like the ones we experience as humans.

   - Ⓐ (as it is now)
   - Ⓑ have strong feelings and emotions
   - Ⓒ have strong feelings and experience powerful emotions,
   - Ⓓ have strong feelings and definitely have emotions,

2. Which of the following is the best version of the underlined portion of this sentence?

   Regardless, scientific consensus on the question of fish emotion <u>is beginning to undergo a shift.</u>

   - Ⓐ (as it is now)
   - Ⓑ is beginning to undergo major shifting.
   - Ⓒ is beginning to undergo a number of shifts.
   - Ⓓ is beginning to shift.

3. Which of the following is the best version of the underlined portion of this sentence?

   These responses seem to be found in <u>most fish.</u>

   - Ⓐ (as it is now)
   - Ⓑ most fish animals.
   - Ⓒ most fish that are animals.
   - Ⓓ most.

 **Wrap-Up**

Instructions
Complete the wrap-up question. If time remains after you've finished, double-check your work.

Passage
(1) When schools of fish gather again after time apart, they will swim around each other while waving their fins and performing elaborate dances. **(2)** Stingrays have been seen frolicking over fields of coral, twirling and flapping their wings, even when ample open ocean is readily available. **(3)** Some have argued that these kinds of behaviors show that fish can feel emotions like joy and delight.

(4) Even advocates for the argument that fish have feelings acknowledge that scientists can easily misidentify what they are seeing with their eyes. **(5)** The shape of a fish's mouth makes it look like it is surprised; it looks that way even when it is excited or in danger. **(6)** Fish are social, communicating underwater using clicks and bubbles. **(7)** Feelings are challenging to understand even in humans, who have the ability to talk about their emotions.

(8) Many oceanographers who devote their time to studying fish behavior have argued that at least some fish, such as triggerfishes and eels, have strong feelings like the ones we experience as humans. **(9)** Other researchers are doubtful. **(10)** They argue that it has not yet been proven that fish feel emotion in any reliable, reproducible scientific experiments.

(11) Regardless, scientific consensus on the question of fish emotion is beginning to undergo a shift. **(12)** Many biologists have accepted that fish most likely have "primary" emotions such as fear or anger. **(13)** These responses seem to be found in most fish. **(14)** For instance, a zebrafish will avoid a part of the tank where it was once shocked even if the shock has been removed. **(15)** Additionally, scientists believe that feelings can be inferred from fishes' changes in activity and eye movement, or even from involuntary responses like scale shedding.

2. Which of the following is the best version of the underlined portion of sentence 4 (reproduced below)?

   Even advocates for the argument that fish have feelings acknowledge that scientists can easily misidentify what they are <u>seeing with their eyes.</u>

   Ⓐ (as it is now)
   Ⓑ seeing.
   Ⓒ seeing with only the help of their eyes.
   Ⓓ giving a quick look.

Combining Sentences

In this chapter, you will learn to combine sentences to form a single sentence that is clear, correct, and concise.

 **Warm-Up**

Instructions

Complete the warm-up question. If time remains after you've finished, double-check your work.

1. Which of the following is the best way to revise and combine the sentences below?

   Democratic government was established in the 1970s. Then more actions were taken to preserve Catalan.

   (A) Democratic government was established in the 1970s, more actions were taken, and Catalan was preserved.

   (B) Democratic government was established in the 1970s, and they took more actions to preserve Catalan.

   (C) In the 1970s, more actions were taken to preserve Catalan because democratic government was established.

   (D) After democratic government was established in the 1970s, more actions were taken to preserve Catalan.

Groundwork

EXERCISE A

Instructions
Work with your teacher to identify instances of unclear pronouns.

First Draft:

1. On the second morning of the battle, the Spartan warriors and the Persian soldiers clashed again. They now outnumbered the enemy by three to one.

Revision #1:

2. On the second morning of the battle, the Spartan warriors and the Persian soldiers clashed again and now outnumbered the enemy by three to one.

Revision #2:

3. The Spartan warriors and the Persian soldiers, who now outnumbered their enemy by three to one, clashed again on the second morning of the battle.

EXERCISE B

Instructions

Review the following sentences. Determine whether each sentence is too wordy, lacking information, or concise. Circle your answer.

First Draft:

4. "Muckraker" was a term referring to journalists who advocated for reform. "Muckraker" was also a word applied to Upton Sinclair, who was a journalist who investigated the unhygienic practices of meatpacking plants.

    This sentence is ...

    ... too wordy.

    ... lacking information.

    ... concise.

Revision #1:

5. "Muckraker" is a term applied to those who advocated for reform, like Upton Sinclair, who was a journalist.

    This sentence is ...

    ... too wordy.

    ... lacking information.

    ... concise.

Revision #2:

6. "Muckraker" was a term for journalists who advocated for reform, like Upton Sinclair, who investigated the unhygienic practices of meatpacking plants.

    This sentence is ...

    ... too wordy.

    ... lacking information.

    ... concise.

EXERCISE C

Instructions
Use the word bank below to connect the two parts of each sentence.

although   after   and   resulting in

7. The lifelong fascination that river travel held for Samuel Clemens inspired his famous pen name,

    Mark Twain, _____ helped him paint a vivid setting for *The Adventures of Huckleberry Finn*.

8. _____ ancient Egyptians rarely named their pet cats, they recorded many affectionate

    names for their dogs, like "Blacky" and "Brave One."

9. _____ Hannibal invaded Rome with war elephants, Romans became terrified of the animals

    and featured them as monsters in bedtime stories for children.

Application

⊘ THE APPROACH

When you are asked to revise and combine two sentences, use the following steps ...

1. Eliminate options with unclear pronouns or misplaced descriptions.
2. Eliminate repetitive terms or unnecessary wordiness.
3. Eliminate answers with illogical connections between ideas.

10. Which of the following best combines the two sentences below?

    Japanese artisans don't discard cracked pottery and instead patch the cracks with gold lacquer. The artisans do this to celebrate the object's history and its "scars."

    (A) They patch the cracks with gold lacquer instead of discarding it, which celebrates the object's history and its "scars."

    (B) When pottery cracks, Japanese artisans do not discard the cracked pottery, and instead they patch the cracks with gold lacquer, and this is so that the artisans can celebrate the object's history and its "scars"

    (C) Instead of discarding cracked pottery, Japanese artisans patch the cracks with gold lacquer in order to celebrate the object's history and its "scars."

    (D) Japanese artisans don't discard cracked pottery, patch the cracks with gold lacquer, and celebrate the object's history and its "scars."

⊘ THE APPROACH

When you are asked to revise and combine two sentences, use the following steps ...

1. Eliminate options with unclear pronouns or misplaced descriptions.
2. Eliminate repetitive terms or unnecessary wordiness.
3. Eliminate answers with illogical connections between ideas.

11. Which answer choice best combines the two sentences below?

Although they lived on separate islands, Pacific Islander tribes often sailed across the sea for friendly visits. They exchanged shell necklaces as a show of good faith.

(A) Even though they lived on separate islands, Pacific Islander tribes often sailed across the sea for friendly visits, but they exchanged shell necklaces as a show of good faith.

(B) Pacific Islander tribes often sailed across the sea for friendly visits, and the tribes of Pacific Islanders that lived on separate islands exchanged shell necklaces as a show of good faith.

(C) Although they lived on separate islands, Pacific Islander tribes often sailed across the sea for friendly visits, exchanged shell necklaces, they showed good faith.

(D) Although they lived on separate islands, Pacific Islander tribes often sailed across the sea for friendly visits and exchanged shell necklaces as a show of good faith.

 **Practice**

Instructions

Complete the practice set. If time remains after you've finished, double-check your work.

1. Which of the following best combines the sentences below?

    Each individual fragment is tiny. Picture by picture, enormous databases of street views are transformed into driving directions.

    (A) Picture by picture, enormous databases of street views are transformed into driving directions, but each individual fragment is tiny.

    (B) Each individual fragment being tiny, enormous databases of street views are transformed into driving directions picture by picture.

    (C) Though each individual fragment is tiny, picture by picture, enormous databases of street views are transformed into driving directions.

    (D) Despite tiny fragments, each individual transforms enormous databases of street views into driving directions.

2. Which of the following best combines the sentences below?

    Junot Díaz wrote The Brief Wondrous Life of Oscar Wao. *The 2008 Pulitzer Prize for Fiction was awarded to Díaz for his novel* The Brief Wondrous Life of Oscar Wao.

    (A) *The Brief Wondrous Life of Oscar Wao*, written by Junot Díaz, and awarded the 2008 Pulitzer Prize for Fiction.

    (B) Junot Díaz wrote *The Brief Wondrous Life of Oscar Wao*, he was awarded the 2008 Pulitzer Prize for Fiction for this novel.

    (C) The 2008 Pulitzer Prize for Fiction was awarded to Junot Díaz for his novel *The Brief Wondrous Life of Oscar Wao*.

    (D) Written by Junot Díaz and awarded the 2008 Pulitzer Prize for Fiction, *The Brief Wondrous Life of Oscar Wao*.

3. Which of the following best combines the sentences below?

    Sonia Sanchez recited her poem "This Is Not a Small Voice." The students were inspired.

    (A) When Sonia Sanchez recited her poem "This Is Not a Small Voice," the students were inspired.

    (B) The students were inspired, Sonia Sanchez recited her poem "This Is Not a Small Voice."

    (C) The poem "This Is Not a Small Voice" recited by Sonia Sanchez, it was inspiring for the students.

    (D) Inspired by the poem "This Is Not a Small Voice," Sonia Sanchez recited for the students.

 **Wrap-Up**

Instructions
Complete the wrap-up question. If time remains after you've finished, double-check your work.

2. Which of the following best combines the sentences below?

Other researchers are doubtful. They argue that it has not yet been proven that fish feel emotion in any reliable, reproducible scientific experiments.

Ⓐ Although they argue that it has not yet been proven that fish feel emotion in any reliable, reproducible scientific experiments, other researchers are doubtful.

Ⓑ Other researchers are doubtful; furthermore, they argue that it has not yet been proven that fish feel emotion in any reliable, reproducible scientific experiments.

Ⓒ Other researchers are doubtful, arguing that it has not yet been proven that fish feel emotion in any reliable, reproducible scientific experiments.

Ⓓ It has not yet been proven that fish feel emotion in any reliable, reproducible scientific experiments, some researchers argue, although they are, admittedly, doubtful.

This page is intentionally left blank.
Content resumes on the next page.

Parallelism

In this chapter, you will be introduced to the concept of parallel structure within sentences and among the elements of lists. In addition, you will practice identifying and correcting errors in parallelism.

🎯 LEARNING TARGETS

1. Recognize the effects of non-parallel structures among equal elements of a list.

2. Identify and correct elements of a sentence that are not parallel in structure.

Warm-Up

Instructions
Complete the warm-up question. If time remains after you've finished, double-check your work.

1. The essence of joy is this: to greet each day as if it were your last, to love, and <u>to be laughing</u>.

   Ⓐ (as it is now)

   Ⓑ for laughing

   Ⓒ to laugh

   Ⓓ laughing

Groundwork

EXERCISE A

Instructions
Revise the following resume skills so that the list maintains parallel structure.

SKILLS | REVISED SKILLS

- Exceptional flexibility

  _____

- I'm very organized

  _____

- Responsible

  _____

- Cooperates with others

  _____

EXERCISE B

Instructions
In the space provided, identify the type of word each portion of the sentence begins with.

It's important to keep your interview answers

1. _____ concise but not so short that you don't get the point across,

2. _____ relevant to the question that was asked, *and*

3. _____ they should be relatable to the interviewer.

Joe was worried about

4. _____ dressing the right way for his interview *and*

5. _____ to ask the right questions.

EXERCISE C

Instructions
Underline the two phrases in each sentence that should be parallel. If a parallelism error occurs, rewrite the corrected sentence in the space provided.

6. Choosing a career that you love means a person never having to work a day in your life. _____

   _____

   _____

7. An enthusiastic candidate makes a better impression and finishes the interview with a better

   chance of getting the job. _____

   _____

8. An enthusiastic candidate makes a better impression, and more likely to get hired if they make a

   positive comment about the company._____

   _____

   _____

Application

✓ THE APPROACH

When you are asked to correct a parallelism error, use the following steps ...

1. Identify the elements of the sentence that need to be parallel.

2. Eliminate answers that do not create parallel structure.

9. Rachel's mother asked her to gather all the leaves in the yard and <u>stuffing them into bags</u> so her father could load them into his truck.

    Ⓐ (as it is now)

    Ⓑ had stuffed them into bags

    Ⓒ could stuff them into bags

    Ⓓ to stuff them into bags

⊘ THE APPROACH

When you are asked to correct a parallelism error, use the following steps ...

1. Identify the elements of the sentence that need to be parallel.

2. Eliminate answers that do not create parallel structure.

10. Swimming is an incredible form of exercise that builds muscle and <u>you can minimize joint pain</u>.

Ⓐ (as it is now)

Ⓑ minimizes joint pain

Ⓒ it can minimize joint pain

Ⓓ minimizing joint pain

 **Practice**

Instructions

Complete the practice set. If time remains after you've finished, double-check your work.

1. Doing large puzzles and <u>when she added to her pottery collection are Anastasia's favorite activities</u> to do inside during the winter.

    Ⓐ (as it is now)

    Ⓑ to add to her pottery collection is Anastasia's favorite activity

    Ⓒ adding to her pottery collection is Anastasia's favorite activity

    Ⓓ adding to her pottery collection are Anastasia's favorite activities

2. The astronauts not only had to adjust to working in a weightless environment but also <u>had to sleep</u> while strapped to a wall of the spaceship.

    Ⓐ (as it is now)

    Ⓑ were sleeping

    Ⓒ slept

    Ⓓ had slept

3. Sweeping the floor and <u>when he folded the laundry are Marco's weekly chores</u> to do at home during the school year.

    Ⓐ (as it is now)

    Ⓑ to fold the laundry is Marco's weekly chore

    Ⓒ folding the laundry is Marco's weekly chore

    Ⓓ folding the laundry are Marco's weekly chores

Wrap-Up

Instructions

Complete the wrap-up question. If time remains after you've finished, double-check your work.

2. The contestants not only had to blindfold themselves to compete in the race but also <u>had to run</u>
    while knee-deep in a puddle of mud.

    - Ⓐ (as it is now)
    - Ⓑ were running
    - Ⓒ ran
    - Ⓓ had ran

This page is intentionally left blank.
Content resumes on the next page.

Misplaced Modifiers

In this chapter, you will correctly identify and place phrases that modify subjects and objects.

🎯 LEARNING TARGETS

1. Evaluate placement of descriptive phrases and the effect it has on meaning and clarity.

2. Identify modifiers and connect them to the element of the sentence they describe.

3. Utilize clarity of meaning as a means for eliminating incorrect answers on the TSIA2.

Warm-Up

Instructions
Complete the warm-up question. If time remains after you've finished, double-check your work.

1. Recognized internationally for her innovative piano compositions, <u>the composer's only musical instruction was her mother</u>, a piano tuner and shop owner.

    Ⓐ the composer's only musical instruction was her mother

    Ⓑ the only instruction the composer received was her mother's

    Ⓒ the composer only received musical instruction that was her mother's

    Ⓓ the composer received her only musical instruction from her mother

Groundwork

EXERCISE A

Instructions

Review the sentence with different placements of the modifier "just" to analyze its effect on the meaning.

1.   **(1)** The teacher **(2)** looked at Zach **(3)** as he came in late to class again.

EXERCISE B

Instructions

Determine the best place to add the modifier to the sentence below. Circle your answer.

Modifier: that was burnt to an absolute crisp

2. The culinary student **(1)** dumped his poor attempt at a homemade pizza **(2)** into the trash can **(3)**.

EXERCISE C

Instructions
Underline the misplaced modifier in each sentence and circle the noun it should describe.

3. He gave cupcakes to his students on napkins.

4. She offered some garlic bread to the man that was dripping with butter.

5. I watched a dog hanging out of his owner's window while driving on the freeway.

Application

⊘ THE APPROACH

When a sentence contains modifiers and the answer choices offer a variety of connecting nouns, use these steps ...

1. Locate the modifying phrase(s).
2. Determine what is being modified.
3. Eliminate answer choices that separate the noun from its modifier.
4. Eliminate answer choices that are unclear.

6. After losing many belongings during a cross-country move, <u>Alexia treasured her last remaining family heirloom</u>, a vintage tea set from China.

   Ⓐ Alexia treasured her last remaining family heirloom
   Ⓑ a treasure of Alexia's was the last remaining family heirloom
   Ⓒ Alexia's treasured family heirloom was the last one remain
   Ⓓ Alexia treasured her family heirloom that was the last one remaining

⊘ THE APPROACH

When a sentence contains modifiers and the answer choices offer a variety of connecting nouns, use these steps ...

1. Locate the modifying phrase(s).
2. Determine what is being modified.
3. Eliminate answer choices that separate the noun from its modifier.
4. Eliminate answer choices that are unclear.

7. A work of historical fiction, <u>the story's heavy research was done by its author</u>, who believed accuracy was the key to writing a good book.

    Ⓐ the story's heavy research was done by its author

    Ⓑ the story had heavy research that was its author's

    Ⓒ the story's heavy research was an author

    Ⓓ the story was heavily researched by its author

 **Practice**

Instructions
Complete the practice set. If time remains after you've finished, double-check your work.

1. Cheered by large crowds of enthusiastic fans, <u>the band owed its popularity to its lead singer</u>, a famous actor known for his role in a recent hit movie.

    Ⓐ the band owed its popularity to its lead singer

    Ⓑ the popularity of the band was its lead singer's

    Ⓒ the band's popularity was its lead singer

    Ⓓ the band owed its popularity that was its lead singer's

2. Nervous before the final round of debate competition, <u>Meena's helpful advice was her speech teacher</u>, an expert in calm breathing techniques.

    Ⓐ Meena's helpful advice was her speech teacher

    Ⓑ the helpful advice Meena got was her speech teacher's

    Ⓒ Meena got helpful advice that was her speech teacher's

    Ⓓ Meena got helpful advice from her speech teacher

3. Buried for thousands of years, <u>the ancient coin's discovery was by a farmer</u>, a local resident who noticed the metal object while working in his field.

    Ⓐ the ancient coin's discovery was by a farmer

    Ⓑ the ancient coin was discovered by a farmer

    Ⓒ the discovery of the ancient coin was a farmer

    Ⓓ the ancient coin had a discovery that was a farmer's

Wrap-Up

Instructions

Complete the wrap-up question. If time remains after you've finished, double-check your work.

2. Praised by the judges for her graceful floor routines, <u>the gymnast's only instruction was her grandmother</u>, a ballroom dancer and choreographer.

- Ⓐ the gymnast's only instruction was her grandmother
- Ⓑ the only instruction the gymnast received was her grandmother's
- Ⓒ the gymnast only received instruction that was her grandmother's
- Ⓓ the gymnast received her only instruction from her grandmother

This page is intentionally left blank.
Content resumes on the next page.

Development

In this chapter, you will practice identifying and eliminating sentences in passages which are off-topic or distract from the meaning of the passage.

🎯 **LEARNING TARGETS**

1. Identify the function of sentences in a paragraph.

2. Keep sentences which add detail or organize passages.

3. Eliminate sentences which distract from the meaning of the passage.

 **Warm-Up**

Instructions
Complete the warm-up question. If time remains after you've finished, double-check your work.

Passage

(1) When schools of fish gather again after time apart, they will swim around each other while waving their fins and performing elaborate dances. **(2)** Stingrays have been seen, frolicking over fields of coral, twirling and flapping their wings, even when ample open ocean is readily available. **(3)** Some have argued that these kinds of behaviors show that fish can feel emotions like joy and delight.

(4) Even advocates for the argument that fish have feelings acknowledge that scientists can easily misidentify what they are seeing. **(5)** The shape of a fish's mouth makes it look like it is surprised; it looks that way even when it is excited or in danger. **(6)** Fish are social, communicating underwater using clicks and bubbles. **(7)** Feelings are challenging to understand even in humans, who have the ability to talk about their emotions.

(8) Many oceanographers who devote their time to studying fish behavior have argued that at least some fish, such as triggerfishes and eels, have strong feelings like the ones we experience as humans. **(9)** Other researchers are doubtful. **(10)** They argue that it has not yet been proven that fish feel emotion in any reliable, reproducible scientific experiments.

(11) Regardless, scientific consensus on the question of fish emotion is beginning to shift. **(12)** Many biologists have accepted that fish most likely have "primary" emotions such as fear or anger. **(13)** These responses seem to be found in most fish. **(14)** For instance, a zebrafish will avoid a part of the tank where it was once shocked even if the shock has been removed. **(15)** Additionally, scientists believe that feelings can be inferred from fishes' changes in activity and eye movement, or even from involuntary responses like scale shedding.

1. Which of the following sentences contains information irrelevant to the passage as a whole and would best be deleted from the passage?

   (A) Sentence 3

   (B) Sentence 6

   (C) Sentence 9

   (D) Sentence 13

Groundwork

EXERCISE A

Instructions
Determine which sentence does not belong in the following passage. Circle your answer.

Passage
(1) The most expensive pizza in the world can be found in a town called Salerno, Italy. (2) A restaurant called Luis XIII offers its customers the opportunity to indulge in a pizza made from a handcrafted, aged pizza dough, which is carefully rolled out and coated in sauce. (3) Toppings range from three different types of expensive caviar to rare grains of pink sea salt from Australia and lobster imported from Norway. (4) What's more is that this pizza is *for delivery*. (5) That's right. (6) A chef will appear at your home, where they will construct and serve this show stopper of a pizza. (7) Strangely enough, famous actor Bill Murray worked as a pizza delivery person before his big break into show business. (8) In total, this pizza will cost someone just over $12,000 to enjoy.

1. Sergio is considering cutting a sentence from his essay, but he can't decide. Should he remove sentence 3 or sentence 7?

　　　　　　Sentence 3　　　　　　　　　Sentence 7

EXERCISE B

Instructions

Review the following reasons why a sentence might need to be deleted as your teacher leads the discussion. Then, match each reason to the underlined sentence from the passage that makes that mistake.

Delete the sentence when	... it blurs the focus of the passage.
	... it contradicts the information in the passage.

Passage

(1) One of the reasons why pizza is such a popular meal is its customizability. (2) Countries, cultures, and even individuals take the essence of what a pizza is and add in their personal tastes to make it into exactly what they crave. (3) For instance, Americans can't stand anchovies and it's the least requested topping in the country. (4) The most popular pizza topping across the U.S. is pepperoni. (5) In Japan, they often top their pizza with mayonnaise, though it is a sweeter variant than what is commonly seen in America. (6) South Africa opened its first Pizza Hut in 2008 thinking that most individuals would eat in the restaurant, but delivery became a much more popular option. (7) Regardless of toppings, pizza remains one of the most universal foods in the world.

2. Sentence _____ blurs the focus of the paragraph.

3. Sentence _____ contradicts information in the paragraph.

 **Application**

⊘ THE APPROACH

When a question asks you which sentence from the passage should be deleted or removed, use these steps ...

1. Determine the main idea of the paragraph or passage.
2. Review each answer choice.
3. Eliminate the sentence that blurs focus or contradicts the passage.

Passage

(1) There is growing concern that public golf courses are a drain on resources and are environmentally unsustainable, especially as the sport has become less popular. (2) According to the National Golf Foundation, only 1.5 million people took up golf in 2011, down from 2.4 million in 2000. (3) Golf can provide a good, low intensity workout in which players burn up to 400 calories an hour. (4) At the same time, golf courses require massive amounts of water and fertilizer to maintain the grass. (5) Due to the decreasing number of golfers, some people feel that having public golf courses is no longer necessary and that the land could be put to better use.

4. Which sentence contains information irrelevant to the passage as a whole and should be deleted?

   (A) Sentence 1
   (B) Sentence 2
   (C) Sentence 3
   (D) Sentence 4

✓ THE APPROACH

When a question asks you which sentence from the passage should be deleted or removed, use these steps …

1. Determine the main idea of the paragraph or passage.
2. Review each answer choice.
3. Eliminate the sentence that blurs focus or contradicts the passage.

Passage

(1) Today, the 19th-century American author Kate Chopin is well known for her controversial novel *The Awakening* and her colorful short stories about life in New Orleans. (2) Her contemporary, George Washington Cable, is also known for his stories set in New Orleans. (3) After falling into obscurity, Chopin's work was rediscovered in the 1960s by Norwegian academic Per Seyersted. (4) Chopin's stories are especially notable for their presentation of issues facing women of the day, such as a lack of independence.

5. Which sentence contains information irrelevant to the passage as a whole and should be deleted?

   (A) Sentence 1

   (B) Sentence 2

   (C) Sentence 3

   (D) Sentence 4

 **Practice**

Instructions
Complete the practice set. If time remains after you've finished, double-check your work.

Passage
(1) Before logging into or buying an item from some websites, you may have been asked to identify everyday objects in a series of images. **(2)** Most internet users have encountered this online security measure, but not many are aware that this widget is essential for training artificial intelligence programs for self-driving vehicles.

(3) These Turing tests—programs designed to distinguish between humans and computers—work because some images are more easily identified by humans than by computers. **(4)** Alan Turing was an English mathematician and an influential thinker in the field of computer science's early days. **(5)** The primary online Turing test, CAPTCHA, is used to block malware, or "bots," from accessing sensitive parts of websites. **(6)** Initially, CAPTCHAs were made up of smudged text the user had to decipher—a difficult task for a robot. **(7)** But by 2014, a team of computer programmers at Waymo, a self-driving car company owned by Google, created a new version of the CAPTCHA that put all these identifications to better use.

(8) In the new version, users are shown a grid of nine images to identify, instead of a snippet of smudged text. **(9)** Some of the images are known by the program and used for comparison. **(10)** But the other images are fragments of street views that computer vision techniques have been unable to recognize. **(11)** The same image fragment is shown to a number of users, and their identifications are compared by the software. **(12)** Once a consensus is found, the software goes on to the next block of unidentified images. **(13)** Image identification technology has applications in diverse fields, ranging from surveillance to cryptography, and even social media.

(14) Globally, 200 million image CAPTCHAs are solved daily. **(15)** Each individual fragment is tiny. **(16)** Picture by picture, enormous databases of street views are transformed into driving directions. **(17)** For example, CAPTCHAs have been used to develop algorithms for the first self-driving taxi service and for the Paris Metro's automated trains, which have been in service since 2019. **(18)** Their construction began in 2012. **(19)** So if you find yourself frustrated with a CAPTCHA, try to remember that you are contributing to the technology that may one day change the way we navigate the modern world.

1. Which of the following sentences contains information irrelevant to the passage as a whole and would best be deleted from the passage?

    (A) Sentence 2
    (B) Sentence 4
    (C) Sentence 5
    (D) Sentence 6

Instructions
Complete the practice set. If time remains after you've finished, double-check your work.

Passage
(1) Before logging into or buying an item from some websites, you may have been asked to identify everyday objects in a series of images. (2) Most internet users have encountered this online security measure, but not many are aware that this widget is essential for training artificial intelligence programs for self-driving vehicles.

(3) These Turing tests—programs designed to distinguish between humans and computers—work because some images are more easily identified by humans than by computers. (4) Alan Turing was an English mathematician and an influential thinker in the field of computer science's early days. (5) The primary online Turing test, CAPTCHA, is used to block malware, or "bots," from accessing sensitive parts of websites. (6) Initially, CAPTCHAs were made up of smudged text the user had to decipher—a difficult task for a robot. (7) But by 2014, a team of computer programmers at Waymo, a self-driving car company owned by Google, created a new version of the CAPTCHA that put all these identifications to better use.

(8) In the new version, users are shown a grid of nine images to identify, instead of a snippet of smudged text. (9) Some of the images are known by the program and used for comparison. (10) But the other images are fragments of street views that computer vision techniques have been unable to recognize. (11) The same image fragment is shown to a number of users, and their identifications are compared by the software. (12) Once a consensus is found, the software goes on to the next block of unidentified images. (13) Image identification technology has applications in diverse fields, ranging from surveillance to cryptography, and even social media.

(14) Globally, 200 million image CAPTCHAs are solved daily. (15) Each individual fragment is tiny. (16) Picture by picture, enormous databases of street views are transformed into driving directions. (17) For example, CAPTCHAs have been used to develop algorithms for the first self-driving taxi service and for the Paris Metro's automated trains, which have been in service since 2019. (18) Their construction began in 2012. (19) So if you find yourself frustrated with a CAPTCHA, try to remember that you are contributing to the technology that may one day change the way we navigate the modern world.

2. Which of the following sentences contains information irrelevant to the passage as a whole and would best be deleted from the passage?

   Ⓐ Sentence 8

   Ⓑ Sentence 10

   Ⓒ Sentence 12

   Ⓓ Sentence 13

Instructions
Complete the practice set. If time remains after you've finished, double-check your work.

Passage
(1) Before logging into or buying an item from some websites, you may have been asked to identify everyday objects in a series of images. **(2)** Most internet users have encountered this online security measure, but not many are aware that this widget is essential for training artificial intelligence programs for self-driving vehicles.

(3) These Turing tests—programs designed to distinguish between humans and computers—work because some images are more easily identified by humans than by computers. **(4)** Alan Turing was an English mathematician and an influential thinker in the field of computer science's early days. **(5)** The primary online Turing test, CAPTCHA, is used to block malware, or "bots," from accessing sensitive parts of websites. **(6)** Initially, CAPTCHAs were made up of smudged text the user had to decipher—a difficult task for a robot. **(7)** But by 2014, a team of computer programmers at Waymo, a self-driving car company owned by Google, created a new version of the CAPTCHA that put all these identifications to better use.

(8) In the new version, users are shown a grid of nine images to identify, instead of a snippet of smudged text. **(9)** Some of the images are known by the program and used for comparison. **(10)** But the other images are fragments of street views that computer vision techniques have been unable to recognize. **(11)** The same image fragment is shown to a number of users, and their identifications are compared by the software. **(12)** Once a consensus is found, the software goes on to the next block of unidentified images. **(13)** Image identification technology has applications in diverse fields, ranging from surveillance to cryptography, and even social media.

(14) Globally, 200 million image CAPTCHAs are solved daily. **(15)** Each individual fragment is tiny. **(16)** Picture by picture, enormous databases of street views are transformed into driving directions. **(17)** For example, CAPTCHAs have been used to develop algorithms for the first self-driving taxi service and for the Paris Metro's automated trains, which have been in service since 2019. **(18)** Their construction began in 2012. **(19)** So if you find yourself frustrated with a CAPTCHA, try to remember that you are contributing to the technology that may one day change the way we navigate the modern world.

3. Which of the following sentences contains information irrelevant to the passage as a whole and would best be deleted from the passage?

   (A) Sentence 15
   (B) Sentence 16
   (C) Sentence 17
   (D) Sentence 18

Wrap-Up

Instructions
Complete the wrap-up question. If time remains after you've finished, double-check your work.

Passage

(1) When schools of fish gather again after time apart, they will swim around each other while waving their fins and performing elaborate dances. (2) Stingrays have been seen frolicking over fields of coral, twirling and flapping their wings, even when ample open ocean is readily available. (3) Some have argued that these kinds of behaviors show that fish can feel emotions like joy and delight. (4) The study of fish is known as "Ichthyology."

(5) Even advocates for the argument that fish have feelings acknowledge that scientists can easily misidentify what they are seeing with their eyes. (6) The shape of a fish's mouth makes it look like it is surprised; it looks that way even when it is excited or in danger. (7) Fish are social, communicating underwater using clicks and bubbles. (8) Feelings are challenging to understand even in humans, who have the ability to talk about their emotions.

(9) Many oceanographers who devote their time to studying fish behavior have argued that at least some fish, such as triggerfish and eels, have strong feelings like the ones we experience as humans. (10) Other researchers are doubtful. (11) They argue that it has not yet been proven that fish feel emotion in any reliable, reproducible scientific experiments.

(12) Regardless, scientific consensus on the question of fish emotion is beginning to shift. (13) Many biologists have accepted that fish most likely have "primary" emotions such as fear or anger. (14) These responses seem to be found in most fish. (15) For instance, a zebrafish will avoid a part of the tank where it was once shocked even if the shock has been removed. (16) Additionally, scientists believe that feelings can be inferred from fishes' changes in activity and eye movement, or even from involuntary responses like scale shedding.

2. Which of the following sentences contains information irrelevant to the passage as a whole and would best be deleted from the passage?

  Ⓐ Sentence 1

  Ⓑ Sentence 2

  Ⓒ Sentence 3

  Ⓓ Sentence 4

Organization

In this chapter, you will evaluate the placement of a sentence within the context of a passage to determine its relevance to the surrounding ideas.

1. Evaluate the organization of ideas in a passage.

2. Determine the best location in an existing passage to add a detail.

Warm-Up

Instructions
Complete the warm-up question. If time remains after you've finished, double-check your work.

Passage

(1) Before logging into or buying an item from some websites, you may have been asked to identify everyday objects in a series of images. **(2)** Most internet users have encountered this online security measure, but not many are aware that this widget is essential for training artificial intelligence programs for self-driving vehicles.

(3) These Turing tests—programs designed to distinguish between humans and computers—work because some images are more easily identified by humans than by computers. **(4)** The primary online Turing test, CAPTCHA, is used to block malware, or "bots," from accessing sensitive parts of websites. **(5)** Initially, CAPTCHAs were made up of smudged text the user had to decipher—a difficult task for a robot.

(6) In the new version, users are shown a grid of nine images to identify, instead of a snippet of smudged text. **(7)** Some of the images are known by the program and used for comparison. **(8)** The same image fragment is shown to a number of users, and their identifications are compared by the software. **(9)** Once a consensus is found, the software goes on to the next block of unidentified images.

(10) Globally, 200 million image CAPTCHAs are solved daily. **(11)** Each individual fragment is tiny. **(12)** Picture by picture, enormous databases of street views are transformed into driving directions. **(13)** For example, CAPTCHAs have been used to develop algorithms for the first self-driving taxi service and for the Paris Metro's automated trains, which have been in service since 2019. **(14)** So if you find yourself frustrated with a CAPTCHA, try to remember that you are contributing to the technology that may one day change the way we navigate the modern world.

1. In context, where would the following sentence best be placed?

    But the other images are fragments of street views that computer vision techniques have been unable to recognize.

    (A) After sentence 7
    (B) After sentence 10
    (C) After sentence 13
    (D) After sentence 14

Groundwork

EXERCISE A

Instructions

Rewrite each detail beneath its relevant topic.

Details

St. Petersburg   Beans   Lens   Zoom   Miami

Portrait   Shanghai   Roasted   Aroma

Cities

Coffee

Photography

EXERCISE B

Instructions

Determine which sentences are irrelevant or out of sequence in the passage. Draw a line through your answers.

Passage

(1) Ferdinand Magellan is most famously credited for being the first person to circumnavigate the world. (2) This expedition—spanning from 1519 to 1522—was not only the first of its kind, but it also provided humans with solid evidence showing that the Earth is not, in fact, flat. (3) Christopher Columbus attempted to sail around the world during his own explorations, but he was unsuccessful. (4) Magellan gained his sailing experience participating in expeditions to Southeast Asia between 1505 and 1512, bringing trade goods back to Portugal. (5) After Magellan returned with evidence of a round Earth, people of that time still did not want to accept that there was no possibility of "sailing off the edge of the world," and it would be more than 100 years until science would provide a more convincing argument.

Instructions

Determine the best location in the following passage to place the provided detail sentence.

Detail:

For example, many of the most popular locations have heavy, rounded arches or thick pillars spanning the front of the home, both characteristics that provide stability to the structures.

Passage

(1) Urban explorers are known for seeking out abandoned buildings and other locales, photographing them, and sharing the stories of those lonely places on social media. **(2)** Many of these individuals feel that urban exploration allows them to connect with the history of a place in a way that they never could in a book or even at a museum.

(3) If you ignore the wear and tear, these old, now-abandoned buildings can be seen as works of art with outstanding examples of craftsmanship and creativity in architecture. **(4)** When these buildings were originally constructed, the architects and designers expected them to be permanent, not lost to ruin. **(5)** Unfortunately, our culture has come to discard old or worn-out places and build new ones, rather than preserving the efforts of the past.

 **Application**

✓ THE APPROACH

When a question asks where you should add a sentence, use these steps ...

1. Review the detail to be added.
2. Test each answer choice placement.
3. Eliminate answer choices that create a disconnect between ideas.

Passage

(1) Today's explorers are professionals with degrees in archaeology and anthropology, high-tech equipment, excellent communication solutions, and teams of people standing by to organize rescue operations. (2) Unlike today's explorers, those who set out 100 years ago had few supplies and little support, and they were primarily amateurs and enthusiasts. (3) Percy Fawcett was an explorer who disappeared into the Amazonian rainforests in 1925. (4) When Fawcett joined the British Royal Geographical Society (RGS), they offered one year of training courses in surveying, observing, and taking notes on the natural world, botany, geology, meteorology, and leadership. (5) Fawcett took this one-year course and aced the final with flying colors.

(6) Fawcett's first assignment with the RGS sent him to the Amazonian rainforests. (7) Bolivia and Brazil were in conflict about the border between their two nations. (8) They appealed to the RGS to send a neutral third party to map the region and determine the border. (9) The RGS chose Percy Fawcett for this 600-mile trek, and in doing so propelled Fawcett toward his legacy.

(10) Percy Fawcett's first expedition to the Amazon was a resounding success. (11) He traveled over 600 miles through the jungle, mapped rivers and national borders, and completed his assignment in half of the time. (12) During this mission, Fawcett heard tales of a city lost in the jungle—a marvelous city full of gold and treasure. (13) Fawcett became obsessed with finding this city, which he called "Z" in his notes. (14) He returned to the region in 1908 and 1909 to measure the Rio Verde on the border between Bolivia and Brazil. (15) In 1910 and 1911, Fawcett was specifically requested by Peru and Bolivia to survey and map the border between those countries. (16) With their help, Fawcett got the chance to lead a non-government expedition to find a lost Inca city in the Andes from 1913 to 1914. (17) Although he didn't find the city, he felt successful in leading the expedition. (18) After World War I, Fawcett got the chance to search for his lost city, Z, in the jungles of Brazil. (19) Finally, in April 1925, Fawcett, his son Jack, and Jack's friend Raleigh set out to search once again for Z. (20) After a telegram in May 1925, the three were ever heard from again.

1. In context, where would the following sentence best be placed?

   Due to the urgency created by this conflict, the Society needed to move swiftly and to select an individual who would no doubt do a thorough job.

   Ⓐ After sentence 4

   Ⓑ After sentence 8

   Ⓒ After sentence 11

   Ⓓ After sentence 14

⊘ THE APPROACH

When a question asks where you should add a sentence, use these steps …

1. Review the detail to be added.
2. Test each answer choice placement.
3. Eliminate answer choices that create a disconnect between ideas.

Passage

(1) Today's explorers are professionals with degrees in archaeology and anthropology, high-tech equipment, excellent communication solutions, and teams of people standing by to organize rescue operations. (2) Unlike today's explorers, those who set out 100 years ago had few supplies and little support, and they were primarily amateurs and enthusiasts. (3) Percy Fawcett was an explorer who disappeared into the Amazonian rainforests in 1925. (4) When Fawcett joined the British Royal Geographical Society (RGS), they offered one year of training courses in surveying, observing, and taking notes on the natural world, botany, geology, meteorology, and leadership. (5) Fawcett took this one-year course and aced the final with flying colors.

(6) Fawcett's first assignment with the RGS sent him to the Amazonian rainforests. (7) Bolivia and Brazil were in conflict about the border between their two nations. (8) They appealed to the RGS to send a neutral third party to map the region and determine the border. (9) The RGS chose Percy Fawcett for this 600-mile trek, and in doing so propelled Fawcett toward his legacy.

(10) Percy Fawcett's first expedition to the Amazon was a resounding success. (11) He traveled over 600 miles through the jungle, mapped rivers and national borders, and completed his assignment in half of the time. (12) During this mission, Fawcett heard tales of a city lost in the jungle—a marvelous city full of gold and treasure. (13) Fawcett became obsessed with finding this city, which he called "Z" in his notes. (14) He returned to the region in 1908 and 1909 to measure the Rio Verde on the border between Bolivia and Brazil. (15) In 1910 and 1911, Fawcett was specifically requested by Peru and Bolivia to survey and map the border between those countries. (16) With their help, Fawcett got the chance to lead a non-government expedition to find a lost Inca city in the Andes from 1913 to 1914. (17) Although he didn't find the city, he felt successful in leading the expedition. (18) After World War I, Fawcett got the chance to search for his lost city, Z, in the jungles of Brazil. (19) Finally, in April 1925, Fawcett, his son Jack, and Jack's friend Raleigh set out to search once again for Z. (20) After a telegram in May 1925, the three were ever heard from again.

2. In context, where would the following sentence best be placed?

   As a result of these successes, Fawcett's status as an explorer and his ability to befriend the local tribes became legendary among local governments.

   Ⓐ After sentence 8

   Ⓑ After sentence 9

   Ⓒ After sentence 12

   Ⓓ After sentence 15

 **Practice**

Instructions

Complete the practice set. If time remains after you've finished, double-check your work.

Passage

(1) These days, Barcelona is the only city in Spain where a majority of the residents speak a regional language: Catalan. **(2)** It is taught to every child. **(3)** And to many adults, it is a source of cultural identity. **(4)** Barcelona differs substantially even from other autonomous regions in Spain like Basque Country, which has a majority Basque (rather than Spanish) population. **(5)** In Barcelona, Catalan and Castilian Spanish are both official languages. **(6)** Yet Catalan, alongside Spanish, is considered a primary language, spoken by 70 percent of Barcelonans. **(7)** In Basque Country, which also has two official languages, Basque is secondary to Spanish.

(8) Historians and anthropologists argue that the decline of this regional language dates back to the union of the Castile and Aragon crowns in the late 15th century. **(9)** However, as the monarchy sought to replace regional languages with Spanish, the territory that ultimately became Barcelona remained autonomous. **(10)** This helped preserve Catalan.

(11) Under General Francisco Franco, who ruled from 1936 to 1975, Catalan suffered. **(12)** General Franco, the son of a naval officer father and Spanish-speaking mother, made it a forbidden language and punished Catalan speakers with imprisonment for their disobedience. **(13)** Democratic government was established in the 1980s. **(14)** Then more actions were taken to preserve Catalan. **(15)** However, not everyone feels confident about Catalan's future, pointing to changes like the growing number of immigrants from Latin America, where Spanish is typically the dominant language, to Barcelona, where Catalan has the upper hand. **(16)** Whether Catalan can continue to grow, or at least hold on, in an increasingly evolving society within an ever-changing world remains an open question.

1. In context, where would the following sentence best be placed?

    The 1993 Constitution made Catalan equivalent to Spanish in Catalonia, and superintendents report that they have thoroughly improved Catalan instruction in grade schools.

    (A) After sentence 1
    (B) After sentence 6
    (C) After sentence 10
    (D) After sentence 14

Instructions

Complete the practice set. If time remains after you've finished, double-check your work.

Passage

(1) In the course of his life, entrepreneur, navigator, and pilot Wiley Post achieved several aviation feats. **(2)** Among them, he is likely best known for one that he achieved as an airplane pilot. **(3)** In 1933, Post managed an unassisted journey around the globe in a single-engine aircraft. **(4)** He was the first person to accomplish this.

(5) On four earlier efforts, Post had piloted a single-engine airplane flight with the goal of traversing the continent. **(6)** These journeys were not completed for a number of reasons. **(7)** The equipment was too damaged for Post to continue the trip safely, and he was compelled to execute a crash landing. **(8)** On another try, a strong headwind forced his plane to land at an Army outpost, where he could refuel.

(9) Post's achievement in 1933 was attributed in part to his use of a modified airplane called the *Winnie Mae.* **(10)** The airplane, launched from New York, permitted Post to voyage over the Atlantic Ocean at a speed of more than a hundred miles an hour. **(11)** Throughout this trip, Post also stayed in touch with ground radar, which helped him to avoid the navigational errors that had plagued others. **(12)** Less than eight days after the airplane's takeoff, Post finished his ground-breaking trip and touched down in Brooklyn.

2. Where in the passage should the following statement be placed?

    Post's 1933 voyage was not his only shot at breaking a record.

    (A) Immediately before sentence 5

    (B) Immediately before sentence 9

    (C) Immediately before sentence 11

    (D) Immediately before sentence 12

3. Where in the passage should the following statement be placed?

    In one attempt, a jealous competitor secretly sabotaged the plane.

    (A) After sentence 3

    (B) After sentence 6

    (C) After sentence 9

    (D) After sentence 11

 Wrap-Up

Instructions

Complete the wrap-up question. If time remains after you've finished, double-check your work.

Passage

(1) Before logging into or buying an item from some websites, you may have been asked to identify everyday objects in a series of images. **(2)** Most internet users have encountered this online security measure, but not many are aware that this widget is essential for training artificial intelligence programs for self-driving vehicles.

(3) These Turing tests—programs designed to distinguish between humans and computers—work because some images are more easily identified by humans than by computers. **(4)** The primary online Turing test, CAPTCHA, is used to block malware, or "bots," from accessing sensitive parts of websites. **(5)** Initially, CAPTCHAs were made up of smudged text the user had to decipher—a difficult task for a robot.

(6) In the new version, users are shown a grid of nine images to identify, instead of a snippet of smudged text. **(7)** Some of the images are known by the program and used for comparison. **(8)** The same image fragment is shown to a number of users, and their identifications are compared by the software. **(9)** Once a consensus is found, the software goes on to the next block of unidentified images.

(10) Globally, 200 million image CAPTCHAs are solved daily. **(11)** Each individual fragment is tiny. **(12)** Picture by picture, enormous databases of street views are transformed into driving directions. **(13)** For example, CAPTCHAs have been used to develop algorithms for the first self-driving taxi service and for the Paris Metro's automated trains, which have been in service since 2019. **(14)** So if you find yourself frustrated with a CAPTCHA, try to remember that you are contributing to the technology that may one day change the way we navigate the modern world.

2. In context, where would the following sentence best be placed?

    But by 2014, a team of computer programmers at Waymo, a self-driving car company owned by Google, created a new version of the CAPTCHA that put all these identifications to better use.

    Ⓐ Before sentence 3

    Ⓑ After sentence 3

    Ⓒ After sentence 4

    Ⓓ After sentence 5

Sentence Revision

In this chapter, you will review and apply a prescribed set of steps that can be used to answer writing-focused questions called Sentence Revision.

Groundwork

EXERCISE A

Instructions

Review the following question as your teacher leads the discussion. Do not answer the question.

Select the best version of the underlined part of the sentence. If you think the original sentence is best, choose the first answer.

1. To enter the tournament, the student or <u>teacher have to</u> pay $10, and all of the proceeds go to help build a new greenhouse.

    Ⓐ teacher have to

    Ⓑ teacher has to

    Ⓒ teacher must have to

    Ⓓ teacher had to

EXERCISE B

Instructions

Review the basic steps for answering a sentence revision question. Put them into the correct sequence by filling in numbers 1–4 in the space provided.

_____ If the sentence sounds wrong, cross off choice A and any choices that repeat the problem.

_____ Use the process of elimination.

_____ Read the sentence.

_____ Compare the remaining answer choices.

 **Application**

⊘ THE APPROACH

When answering a sentence revision question on the TSIA2, use these steps ...

1. Read the sentence.
2. If it sounds wrong, cross off choice A and any choices that repeat the problem.
3. Compare the remaining choices.
4. Use the process of elimination.

1. To enter the tournament, the student or <u>teacher have to</u> pay $10, and all of the proceeds go to help build a new greenhouse.

   Ⓐ teacher have to
   Ⓑ teacher has to
   Ⓒ teacher must have to
   Ⓓ teacher had to

✓ THE APPROACH

When answering a sentence revision question on the TSIA2, use these steps ...

1. Read the sentence.
2. If it sounds wrong, cross off choice A and any choices that repeat the problem.
3. Compare the remaining choices.
4. Use the process of elimination.

2. <u>Many people</u> think it to be a myth or a hoax, some truly believe they have seen it.

    (A) Many people

    (B) Although many people

    (C) Groups

    (D) Research shows we

 **Practice**

Instructions

Complete the practice set. If time remains after you've finished, double-check your work.

1. <u>With the advancement of identity theft, and some unsuspecting customers being</u> in very real danger.

    Ⓐ With the advancement of identity theft, and some unsuspecting customers being

    Ⓑ With the advancement of identity theft, some unsuspecting customers are

    Ⓒ With identity theft being how it is, some unsuspecting customers being

    Ⓓ Identity theft being how it is, thus some unsuspecting customers being

2. He can grow his own food, and he knows which kinds of wild berries and plants <u>are</u> safe to eat.

    Ⓐ are

    Ⓑ is

    Ⓒ being

    Ⓓ that is

3. Seahorses eat <u>with the use of</u> their snouts to suck up plankton or crustaceans, and they use their tails to hook onto seagrass or coral.

    Ⓐ with the use of

    Ⓑ in using

    Ⓒ by using

    Ⓓ for use of

Subject–Verb Agreement

In this chapter, you will review the concept of grammatical number and learn how to correct subject-verb agreement errors.

🎯 LEARNING TARGETS

1. Identify the subject of a sentence and determine whether it is singular or plural.

2. Match the subject of a sentence to its correct verb form.

3. Utilize your instincts as a strategy for eliminating incorrect answers.

Warm-Up

Instructions

Complete the warm-up question. If time remains after you've finished, double-check your work.

1. White Sands, in New Mexico, <u>are</u> the largest dune field in the United States.

   Ⓐ are

   Ⓑ they are

   Ⓒ being

   Ⓓ is

Groundwork

EXERCISE A

Instructions
Refer to the following phrases as your teacher leads the discussion.

1. _____ The ballerinas

2. _____ The lion

Write an "S" next to the underline{s}ingular nouns. Write a "P" next to the underline{p}lural nouns.

3. _____ One of the ice cubes

4. _____ The scientists working for NASA

5. _____ The audience at the concert

EXERCISE B

Instructions
Refer to the following sentences as your teacher leads the discussion.

6. The ballerinas (dances / dance).

7. The lion (roars / roar).

Circle the verb that matches the subject in number.

8. One of the ice cubes (melts / melt).

9. The scientists working for NASA (has / have) degrees in engineering.

10. The audience at the concert (cheers / cheer).

EXERCISE C

Instructions
Refer to the following sentence as your teacher leads the discussion.

The artists on the bench in the park paints portraits of the people around them.

11. Write the subject and verb by themselves: _____ _____

12. Write the new, corrected subject and verb: _____ _____

Application

⊘ THE APPROACH

When you are asked to correct a subject-verb agreement error, use the following steps ...

1. Match the underlined verb to its subject.
2. Cross out everything between the subject and verb.
3. Choose the verb that matches the subject in number.

Instructions
Refer to the following question as your teacher leads the discussion.

13. According to the meteorologist on our local news station, the storm that started east of the mountains <u>represent</u> a threat.

   Ⓐ represent
   Ⓑ represents
   Ⓒ representing
   Ⓓ it represented

✓ THE APPROACH

When you are asked to correct a subject-verb agreement error, use the following steps ...

1. Match the underlined verb to its subject.
2. Cross out everything between the subject and verb.
3. Choose the verb that matches the subject in number.

Instructions
Refer to the following question as your teacher leads the discussion.

14. Not one of the adults bustling around the kitchen and shouting orders <u>are</u> the host who actually planned the dinner party.

　Ⓐ　are

　Ⓑ　being

　Ⓒ　is

　Ⓓ　they are

Practice

Instructions

Complete the practice set. If time remains after you've finished, double-check your work.

1. Yosemite Falls, in California, <u>are</u> the tallest waterfall in the United States.

    Ⓐ are

    Ⓑ they are

    Ⓒ being

    Ⓓ is

2. The class, in raincoats, <u>were</u> waiting to go outside for recess.

    Ⓐ were

    Ⓑ it was

    Ⓒ being

    Ⓓ was

3. Unlike their cousin the zebra, horses do not have striped coats but instead <u>is</u> taller with long manes and tails, shorter ears, curved backs, and strong, muscular legs.

    Ⓐ is

    Ⓑ they is

    Ⓒ are

    Ⓓ they are

⭐ Wrap-Up

Instructions

Complete the wrap-up question. If time remains after you've finished, double-check your work.

2. Unlike their cousin the moose, deer do not have broad antlers but instead <u>is</u> leaner, with narrow antlers and slender bodies, small snouts, light fur, and short, pointed ears.

   Ⓐ is

   Ⓑ they is

   Ⓒ are

   Ⓓ they are

This page is intentionally left blank.
Content resumes on the next page.

Verb Tense

In this chapter, you will review verb tenses and determine the appropriate verb tense in the context of sentences. You will choose the best verb tense to edit sentences.

🎯 **LEARNING TARGETS**

1. Identify the tense of a verb.

2. Utilize existing verbs and context clues to determine the correct tense of a verb.

Warm-Up

Instructions
Complete the warm-up question. If time remains after you've finished, double-check your work.

1. Most cellphones have short lifespans, becoming unusable once their operating systems or their parts <u>were</u> outdated.

   (A) were

   (B) will be

   (C) are

   (D) being

Groundwork

EXERCISE A

Instructions
Highlight or underline the verb in each sentence. Circle the correct verb tense.

1. You will be on the right path to success.

   past   present   future

2. You were on the right path to success.

   past   present   future

3. You are on the right path to success.

   past   present   future

EXERCISE B

Instructions
Fill in the blanks with an ongoing verb that best completes the sentence.

PRESENT TENSE

4. She **looks** into her crystal ball.

PRESENT ONGOING TENSE

5. At the moment, she **is looking** into her crystal ball.

PAST ONGOING TENSE

6. She _____ into her crystal ball while I waited patiently.

FUTURE ONGOING TENSE

7. When I go in for my appointment tomorrow, she _____ into her crystal ball.

EXERCISE C

Instructions
Use context clues to select the verb that best completes the sentence from the options below. Circle your answer.

8. My psychic predicted good things in my future, and since no one won the big jackpot yesterday,

    I now fully _____ that I will hit the jackpot later this evening.

    was expecting   am expecting   expect

Application

⊘ THE APPROACH

When deciding which tense of a verb best completes a sentence, follow these steps …

1. Find the other verbs in the sentence and identify their tense.

2. Test the verb that matches the existing verbs.

3. If there are no other verbs or if the verbs vary in tense, use context clues.

9. The psychic on the hotline told me my fortune last week, and I <u>am believing</u> everything she said; that was a big mistake.

- Ⓐ am believing
- Ⓑ have believed
- Ⓒ believed
- Ⓓ will believe

⊘ THE APPROACH

When deciding which tense of a verb best completes a sentence, follow these steps ...

1. Find the other verbs in the sentence and identify their tense.
2. Test the verb that matches the existing verbs.
3. If there are no other verbs or if the verbs vary in tense, use context clues.

10. Prior to the 8th century B.C., the *Pythia* <u>was</u> one of the most famous oracles of the time, delivering prophecies from the god Apollo.

   Ⓐ was
   Ⓑ being
   Ⓒ have been
   Ⓓ will be

 **Practice**

Instructions

Complete the practice set. If time remains after you've finished, double-check your work.

1. Most sloths are lazy, becoming active only when their lives or their cubs <u>were</u> threatened.

    (A) were

    (B) will be

    (C) are

    (D) being

2. By the early 2000s, the World Wide Web <u>had connected</u> once-isolated rural towns with urban city centers.

    (A) had connected

    (B) had been connecting

    (C) is connecting

    (D) connected

3. By 2007, the world financial crisis <u>had been throwing</u> once-thriving countries into economic turmoil.

    (A) had been throwing

    (B) is throwing

    (C) had thrown

    (D) threw

Wrap-Up

Instructions

Complete the wrap-up question. If time remains after you've finished, double-check your work.

2. By the early 1990s, global capital <u>is developing</u> the once-industrial city into an international tech hub.

    Ⓐ is developing

    Ⓑ had been developing

    Ⓒ developed

    Ⓓ had developed

This page is intentionally left blank.
Content resumes on the next page.

Pronoun-Antecedent Agreement

In this chapter, you will recognize pronouns, identify antecedents, and ensure that they agree in gender, number, and person.

🎯 **LEARNING TARGETS**

1. Identify the antecedent of a pronoun.

2. Verify that a pronoun matches its antecedent in number, gender, and point of view.

3. Eliminate incorrect answer choices using the *Sounds Wrong Is Wrong* strategy.

 **Warm-Up**

Instructions

Complete the warm-up question. If time remains after you've finished, double-check your work.

Passage

(1) Historians and anthropologists argue that the decline of the Catalan language dates back to the union of the Castile and Aragon crowns in the late 15th century. (2) However, as the monarchy sought to replace regional languages with Spanish, the territory that ultimately became Barcelona remained autonomous. (3) This helped preserve Catalan.

1. In context, which of the following best replaces "This" in sentence 3 (reproduced below)?

   This helped preserve Catalan.

   Ⓐ This independence

   Ⓑ This region

   Ⓒ This monarchy

   Ⓓ This system

Groundwork

EXERCISE A

Instructions
Refer to the following passage as your teacher leads the discussion.

Passage
    Years ago, I read a book called *The Giver* by Lois Lowry. The main character of the story, a 12-year-old boy named Jonas, lives in a strictly controlled futuristic society. Jonas lives in a house with Jonas's parents and little sister, Lily. Despite the advanced technology, Jonas rides Jonas's bike everywhere Jonas goes. Jonas is assigned a job which Jonas goes to every day. Jonas learns how Jonas's community works and that the community may not be as perfect as the community seems.

1. Draw a line to match each noun to the pronoun it could be replaced with.

    Jonas   he

    Jonas's   it

    The community   his

2. Read the following sentence. Underline the two pronouns and circle their antecedent.

    Jonas rides his bike everywhere he goes.

EXERCISE B

Instructions
Circle the pronoun that matches the antecedent in *number*.

3. I love burritos because _____ never judge(s) me.

   it   they

4. I love a good burrito because _____ never judge(s) me.

   it   they

Instructions
Circle the pronoun that matches the antecedent in *gender*.

5. A cupcake is a muffin that believes _____ has witnessed a miracle.

   it   he

6. Emilio told me _____ believes cupcakes are miracle muffins.

   it   he

Instructions
Circle the pronoun that best matches the antecedent in *point of view*.

7. Before, Eliza would just 'crastinate, but after a while, _____ went pro.

   she   you

8. If you are good at 'crastinating, eventually _____ can go pro.

   it   you

Application

⊘ THE APPROACH

When you are challenged to find the pronoun that best agrees with an antecedent, follow these steps ...

1. Find the antecedent to the underlined pronoun.
2. Eliminate choices that do not match in number, gender, or point of view.

9. Watercolor paints, which are often created using a natural pigment, have a translucent appearance when <u>they</u> are painted onto a surface.

   Ⓐ they

   Ⓑ we

   Ⓒ it

   Ⓓ she

⊘ THE APPROACH

When you are challenged to find the pronoun that best agrees with an antecedent, follow these steps ...

1. Find the antecedent to the underlined pronoun.
2. Eliminate choices that do not match in number, gender, or point of view.

10. Many people who attend movies find <u>it</u> to be an enjoyable pastime.

   (A) it
   (B) they
   (C) them
   (D) him

Practice

Instructions
Complete the practice set. If time remains after you've finished, double-check your work.

1. An octopus, which swims with its arms, can expel a jet of water from <u>their</u> body cavity when under threat.

   (A) their

   (B) his

   (C) one's

   (D) its

2. Damhsa, commonly known as Irish stepdance, is a style of dance in which individuals or groups of dancers, moving <u>any part of your bodies except your</u> arms, perform complicated foot movements and jumps.

   (A) any part of your bodies except your

   (B) your body, any part except those

   (C) their bodies, any part of them except

   (D) any part of their bodies except their

3. The children in the class showed <u>one's</u> interest in the presentation by asking the park ranger many questions about her job.

   (A) one's

   (B) their

   (C) its

   (D) our

 **Wrap-Up**

Instructions

Complete the wrap-up question. If time remains after you've finished, double-check your work.

2. Fan fiction, or "fanfic" for short, is a type of literature in which an admirer of a book, using <u>any aspect of your story besides your</u> exact plot, writes a new story and shares it online for free.

   Ⓐ any aspect of your story besides your

   Ⓑ your story, any aspect besides your

   Ⓒ its story, any aspect besides

   Ⓓ any aspect of its story besides its

Possessive Nouns

In this chapter, you will distinguish between possessive and non-possessive singular and plural nouns.

🎯 **LEARNING TARGETS**

1. Determine whether a noun should show possession of another element in a sentence.

2. Use apostrophes to indicate possession.

Warm-Up

Instructions

Complete the warm-up question. If time remains after you've finished, double-check your work.

1. Some such films aim to portray many <u>Americans' ideal's</u> from a specific era.

    (A) Americans' ideal's

    (B) American's ideal's

    (C) Americans ideal's

    (D) Americans' ideals

Groundwork

Instructions

Work with your teacher to evaluate the following phrases.

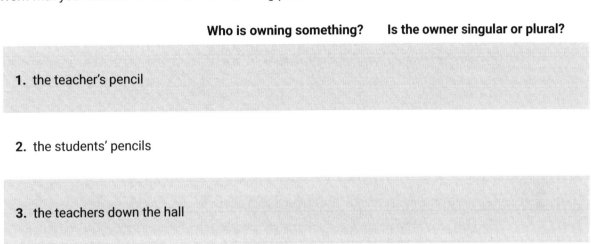

	Who is owning something?	Is the owner singular or plural?
1. the teacher's pencil		
2. the students' pencils		
3. the teachers down the hall		

EXERCISE B

Instructions

Circle the subject of each sentence. Then, label the sentence based on whether the subject of the sentence contains a **possessive (PO)** or **plural (PL)** noun. If it's possessive, add an apostrophe in the appropriate location.

_____ **4.** A snails nap can last up to three years.

_____ **5.** Kangaroos are not able to walk backward.

_____ **6.** A dogs nose print is like a human's fingerprint; each nose print is unique to its owner.

_____ **7.** Zebras stripes act as a natural bug repellent.

_____ **8.** Elephants are one of the few mammalian species that cannot jump.

Application

✓ THE APPROACH

When you are asked to correct a sentence with a possession error, use the following steps ...

1. Find the possessive noun, if there is one.
2. Determine whether the noun is singular or plural.
3. Eliminate choices that don't punctuate the possessive noun correctly.

9. Unfortunately for the nursing staff, the doctor and the anesthesiologist frequently disagreed about <u>patients treatments</u>.

   Ⓐ patients treatments
   Ⓑ patients' treatments
   Ⓒ patients treatments'
   Ⓓ patients' treatments'

⊘ THE APPROACH

When you are asked to correct a sentence with a possession error, use the following steps ...

1. Find the possessive noun, if there is one.
2. Determine whether the noun is singular or plural.
3. Eliminate choices that don't punctuate the possessive noun correctly.

10. After comparing their <u>class' schedules</u>, Tia and Casey realized that they wouldn't be able to eat lunch together this year.

   Ⓐ class' schedules

   Ⓑ class schedules'

   Ⓒ class's schedules

   Ⓓ class schedules

 **Practice**

Instructions

Complete the practice set. If time remains after you've finished, double-check your work.

1. <u>One of the farm's roosters crows</u> all morning long, and it wakes us up.

   Ⓐ One of the farm's roosters crows

   Ⓑ One of the farms rooster's crows

   Ⓒ One of the farm's rooster's crows

   Ⓓ One of the farms roosters crows

2. So many stories begin to reveal many <u>citizen's experience's</u> from that time period.

   Ⓐ citizen's experience's

   Ⓑ citizens' experiences

   Ⓒ citizens experience's

   Ⓓ citizen's experiences

3. A howdunit always offers a clear picture of who the guilty party is but keeps the <u>stories character's</u> in the dark about how the killer did it.

   Ⓐ stories character's

   Ⓑ story's characters

   Ⓒ stories' character's

   Ⓓ stories' characters

Wrap-Up

Instructions
Complete the wrap-up question. If time remains after you've finished, double-check your work.

2. A biopic often explores a new perspective on a well-known historical figure to keep the <u>films'</u> <u>viewers</u> engaged about a familiar subject.

    (A) films' viewers

    (B) film's viewers

    (C) film's viewers'

    (D) films viewers'

Transitions

In this chapter, you will learn how to use transition words and phrases to connect ideas within and between sentences.

🎯 LEARNING TARGETS

1. Determine the type of relationship between two elements in a sentence or passage.

2. Select an appropriate transition to connect ideas in a relationship.

3. Categorize transitions to eliminate incorrect answers on transition questions on the TSIA2.

 **Warm-Up**

Instructions

Complete the warm-up question. If time remains after you've finished, double-check your work.

1. Casey had to buy some new footwear <u>with her shoes being</u> eaten by her dog.

    (A) with her shoes being

    (B) although her shoes were

    (C) whereas her shoes were

    (D) because her shoes had been

Groundwork

EXERCISE A

Instructions

Sort the transitions from the word bank into their correct categories.

although	specifically	in addition	as a result	to illustrate
in conclusion	first	on the other hand	similarly	in the end
in fact	however	consequently	for example	in essence

Transition Categories

1. CONTRAST

_____

_____

_____

4. ILLUSTRATION or SUPPORT

_____

_____

_____

2. ADDITION or EMPHASIS

_____

_____

_____

5. SUMMARY

_____

_____

_____

3. CAUSE/EFFECT or SEQUENCE

_____

_____

_____

EXERCISE B

Instructions
Choose the best transition to complete each sentence.

after that   alternatively   for instance   in fact

6. If you find a doll in the toy section of Target, you might think it's cute; _____, if you find an old, cracked-face doll in the attic, you might want to destroy it in the nearest fire.

7. Benjamin Franklin was pretty surprised when he discovered electricity; _____, you could say he was shocked.

8. The teacher wrote the solution to the math problem on the window; _____, everything was clear.

9. They say music is really good for your brain, but I'm not sold on the idea; _____, if a piano falls on my head, I'm pretty sure my brain won't like it.

Application

⊘ THE APPROACH

When you are asked to determine the appropriate transition to make a connection between ideas, use the following steps ...

1. Determine the relationship between the ideas before and after the transition.
2. Eliminate answers that don't make the right bridge between the ideas.

10. A judge and an English teacher have different responsibilities. <u>Subsequently</u>, they do have one thing in common: lots of sentences.

    Ⓐ Subsequently

    Ⓑ However

    Ⓒ In short

    Ⓓ For example

⊘ THE APPROACH

When you are asked to determine the appropriate transition to make a connection between ideas, use the following steps ...

1. Determine the relationship between the ideas before and after the transition.

2. Eliminate answers that don't make the right bridge between the ideas.

11. Jacob had to move out of his apartment <u>while he couldn't afford</u> the rent anymore.

- Ⓐ while he couldn't afford
- Ⓑ despite the fact that he couldn't afford
- Ⓒ since he couldn't afford
- Ⓓ whereas he couldn't afford

 **Practice**

Instructions

Complete the practice set. If time remains after you've finished, double-check your work.

1. Miranda had to visit the doctor <u>with her shoulder pain increasing</u> for three months.

    Ⓐ with her shoulder pain increasing

    Ⓑ although her shoulder pain increased

    Ⓒ whereas her shoulder pain increased

    Ⓓ because her shoulder pain had increased

2. Michael had to finish his homework <u>with it being</u> due yesterday.

    Ⓐ with it being

    Ⓑ though it was

    Ⓒ while it was

    Ⓓ because it was

3. Alexander only used his microwave <u>until the repairman</u> fixed his oven.

    Ⓐ until the repairman

    Ⓑ thus the repairman

    Ⓒ consequently the repairman

    Ⓓ because the repairman

 **Wrap-Up**

Instructions

Complete the wrap-up question. If time remains after you've finished, double-check your work.

2. Cassandra had yet to return her father's call <u>with him having called</u> her over two weeks ago.

    Ⓐ with him having called

    Ⓑ nevertheless he called

    Ⓒ even though he called

    Ⓓ because he had called

Coordinating Conjunctions

In this chapter, you will review coordinating conjunctions and explore the process of using these connecting words to bridge independent clauses into compound sentences.

🎯 **LEARNING TARGETS**

1. Recall the seven coordinating conjunctions.

2. Distinguish between dependent and independent clauses.

3. Use a coordinating conjunction and appropriate punctuation to create a compound sentence.

Warm-Up

Instructions

Complete the warm-up question. If time remains after you've finished, double-check your work.

1. Early audio production was limited to mono recordings, <u>therefore</u> stereo sound arrived with the emergence of "talkie" sound films in the early 1930s.

    Ⓐ therefore

    Ⓑ however

    Ⓒ when

    Ⓓ but

Groundwork

EXERCISE A

Instructions
Read through the passage and identify the seven coordinating conjunctions that make up FANBOYS.

Passage
Listen. I'm not saying that I'm the best athlete out there, but I can hold my own in gym class. In fact, I can keep pace with the best of them, <u>for</u> I'm a runner at heart. I don't know if it's my competitive nature that keeps me moving, or maybe there's just nothing quite like the feeling of the mental clarity that comes with a long-distance run.

The other day, I was in said gym class, and we were doing laps around the basketball court. Our gym teacher, Mr. Jordan, was standing on the sidelines with his ever-present stopwatch. I had fallen into a good rhythm and was faster than most of my classmates, so I just maneuvered around them when I'd get close.

I wasn't thinking about anything, nor was I focusing on what was in front of me. As I steered myself around a classmate, BAM! I smacked right into a basketball pole. It didn't hurt too much in the moment, yet when I realized I'd lost about three minutes of time somewhere, I knew I'd hurt my head pretty badly. Sure enough, the ER doctor would tell me a few hours later that I'd given myself a concussion.

F → ____ ____ ____

A → ____ ____ ____

N → ____ ____ ____

B → ____ ____ ____

O → ____ ____

Y → ____ ____ ____

S → ____ ____

EXERCISE B

Instructions

Label each clause as either independent (I) or dependent (D).

1. Even though it was raining cats and dogs.   _____

2. I really missed the boat on that one.   _____

3. Because she was the one calling the shots.   _____

4. It's the opposite of having a green thumb.   _____

5. He went out on a limb for me.   _____

EXERCISE C

Instructions

Identify whether the clauses in the sentence are independent (I) or dependent (D). Then, add a coordinating conjunction to the appropriate sentence.

6. It doesn't challenge you, _____ it's not going to change you.

7. If it doesn't challenge you, _____ it's not going to change you.

Application

⊘ THE APPROACH

When a question contains a sentence with two clauses and the answer choices contain connecting words, use these steps …

1. Determine whether the clauses are dependent or independent.
2. Eliminate inappropriate connecting words.
3. Compare the remaining choices and select the one that best fits the sentence.

8. Money can't buy happiness, <u>for</u> it's hard to be sad on a jet ski.

  Ⓐ for

  Ⓑ however

  Ⓒ but

  Ⓓ or

✓ THE APPROACH

When a question contains a sentence with two clauses and the answer choices contain connecting words, use these steps …

1. Determine whether the clauses are dependent or independent.

2. Eliminate inappropriate connecting words.

3. Compare the remaining choices and select the one that best fits the sentence.

---

9. Although this may kill me, <u>and it</u> could make me stronger.

    Ⓐ   and it

    Ⓑ   otherwise it

    Ⓒ   or it

    Ⓓ   it

 **Practice**

Instructions

Complete the practice set. If time remains after you've finished, double-check your work.

1. Early automobiles only had side-door mirrors, <u>since</u> larger reflectors were installed after the introduction of the gasoline engine in the early 1900s.

   Ⓐ since

   Ⓑ however

   Ⓒ as

   Ⓓ but

2. The postal railway system delivered mail across the United States for decades, <u>therefore</u> mail trucks replaced mail trains in the late 1970s.

   Ⓐ therefore

   Ⓑ however

   Ⓒ when

   Ⓓ but

3. Even though Miguel played baseball last season, <u>but he</u> tried out for the tennis team this year.

   Ⓐ but he

   Ⓑ but

   Ⓒ he had

   Ⓓ he

⭐ Wrap-Up

Instructions

Complete the wrap-up question. If time remains after you've finished, double-check your work.

2. While Hector loved cheeseburgers as a teenager, <u>but he</u> decided to become a vegetarian as an adult.

- Ⓐ but he
- Ⓑ but
- Ⓒ he had
- Ⓓ he

This page is intentionally left blank.
Content resumes on the next page.

Sentence Formation

In this chapter, you will review and practice dependent and independent clauses with a focus on subordinating conjunctions and how they indicate the beginning of a dependent clause.

🎯 LEARNING TARGETS

1. Differentiate between complete and incomplete sentences.

2. Use semicolons and subordinate conjunctions to connect two independent clauses.

3. Eliminate verbals that create incomplete sentence structures.

 **Warm-Up**

Instructions

Complete the warm-up question. If time remains after you've finished, double-check your work.

1. The Bergen Dice, which became notorious for its ability to help its user obtain an unfair <u>advantage, discovered by</u> archeologists exploring villages of Norway dating back to the Middle Ages.

   (A) advantage, discovered by

   (B) advantage, to be discovered by

   (C) advantage, having been discovered by

   (D) advantage, was discovered by

Groundwork

EXERCISE A

Instructions
Determine whether the following sentences are complete or incomplete. Circle your answer.

1. Komodo dragons, which were once thought to be venomous, have so much bacteria in their mouths that their prey dies from infection rather than damage from the attack.

    complete   incomplete

2. A certain species of snail, found in parts of eastern Russia as well as Japan, known for throwing their shells at predators as a means of protection.

    complete   incomplete

EXERCISE B

Instructions

Determine which of the following sentences is complete. Circle the complete sentence.

3. Sloths often mistaking their arms for branches and falling out of trees.

4. Sloths often to mistake their arms for branches and to fall out of trees.

5. Sloths often mistake their arms for branches and fall out of trees.

EXERCISE C

Instructions

Determine whether the clauses of each sentence should be separated by a comma or a semicolon.

6. Hummingbirds are able to flap their wings at 200 times per second they need to eat up to eight times their own body weight every day to compensate.

7. Because turkeys are so mesmerized by rain they will often spend upwards of 30 minutes staring at the sky turkey farmers must take caution because turkeys often drown by doing this.

Application

✓ **THE APPROACH**

When you encounter a writing question that contains a mix of verbals and verbs in the answer choices, use these steps ...

1. Determine whether the clause is missing a complete verb.
2. If it is, select a verb that appropriately completes the sentence.
3. If it isn't, select a verbal that appropriately completes the sentence.

8. The young explorer, aware of the many obstacles that lay in her <u>path, embarked</u> on her adventure with a determination to succeed.

    Ⓐ path, embarked
    Ⓑ path, she embarked
    Ⓒ path, embarking
    Ⓓ path, to embark

⊘ THE APPROACH

When you encounter a writing question that contains a mix of verbals and verbs in the answer choices, use these steps ...

1. Determine whether the clause is missing a complete verb.
2. If it is, select a verb that appropriately completes the sentence.
3. If it isn't, select a verbal that appropriately completes the sentence.

9. Because they had been working for hours, the students decided to take a <u>break the group knew</u> that pushing themselves to a mental breaking point wouldn't be helpful anyway.

    Ⓐ break the group knew

    Ⓑ break and the group knowing

    Ⓒ break; the group knew

    Ⓓ break, the group had known

 **Practice**

Instructions

Complete the practice set. If time remains after you've finished, double-check your work.

1. Now that computers are becoming more popular in classrooms, teachers are taking advantage of the <u>opportunity, students were insisting</u> that the update has improved their daily experiences.

    Ⓐ opportunity, students were insisting

    Ⓑ opportunity and students insist

    Ⓒ opportunity students insist

    Ⓓ opportunity; students insist

2. The Hope Diamond, which became part of the English crown jewels before being shipped to <u>France, purchased by</u> Pierre Cartier for an American heiress in 1910.

    Ⓐ France, purchased by

    Ⓑ France, having been purchased by

    Ⓒ France, was purchased by

    Ⓓ France, to be purchased by

3. Ryan loves video games so much <u>that he will not play</u> anything else when video games are an option.

    Ⓐ that he will not play

    Ⓑ that not playing

    Ⓒ to not play

    Ⓓ not to play

Wrap-Up

Instructions
Complete the wrap-up question. If time remains after you've finished, double-check your work.

2. Despite its dilapidated condition, the sculpture was widely beloved by the <u>community; everyone agreed</u> that it was a wonderful example of late-modernist art.

    Ⓐ community; everyone agreed

    Ⓑ community everyone agreed

    Ⓒ community and everyone agreeing

    Ⓓ community, everyone was agreed

This page is intentionally left blank.
Content resumes on the next page.

The 4 C's

In this chapter, you will learn how to strategically eliminate incorrect answers based on the 4 C's: Correct, Consistent, Clear, and Concise.

Groundwork

EXERCISE A

Instructions

Review the following question as your teacher leads the discussion. Do not answer the question.

Select the best version of the underlined part of the sentence. If you think the original sentence is best, choose the first answer.

1. The children thought that their father was being serious when he told them that the word "gullible" is not in the dictionary.

   (A) serious when he told
   (B) serious he told
   (C) serious, he telling
   (D) serious, him telling

EXERCISE B

Instructions

Write the letter of each definition next to its matching term.

1. ____ Correct

    A. The answer presents ideas in a logical manner.

2. ____ Consistent

    B. The answer is brief but comprehensive.

3. ____ Clear

    C. The answer maintains correct verb tense, parallel structure, and point of view.

4. ____ Concise

    D. The answer does not contain or create any grammar or punctuation errors.

EXERCISE C

Instructions
Use the first C (Correct) to eliminate incorrect answers.

5. A pair of runners whip by me, assaulting the quiet with short steps that splash through the <u>water,</u> I love to run, but today it is time to appreciate the serenity of this world.

    Ⓐ water,

    Ⓑ water and

    © water

    Ⓓ water;

Application

⊘ THE APPROACH

When answering a writing question that does not actually contain a question, use these steps ...

1. Eliminate answers that are not correct, consistent, clear, and concise.
2. If more than one option remains, select the answer that sounds the most natural.

Instructions

Use the second C (Consistent) to eliminate incorrect answers.

6. I walk at a decrepit pace; the soft sand squeaks peacefully beneath my feet. <u>I hear</u> the calls of the seagulls above and the crashing of waves in the background. I feel the silky breeze slip quietly across the coast.

    Ⓐ I hear
    Ⓑ You can hear
    Ⓒ One can hear
    Ⓓ While hearing

⊘ THE APPROACH

When answering a writing question that does not actually contain a question, use these steps ...

1. Eliminate answers that are not correct, consistent, clear, and concise.

2. If more than one option remains, select the answer that sounds the most natural.

Instructions

Use the third C (Clear) and fourth C (Concise) to eliminate answer choices.

7. Throughout human history, people of various cultures and religions around the world have developed their own <u>stories regarding</u> rivers.

   Ⓐ stories regarding

   Ⓑ stories to

   Ⓒ stories which they connected to

   Ⓓ stories, related to

 **Practice**

Instructions
Complete the practice set. If time remains after you've finished, double-check your work.

1. According to researchers, many of the vast deserts of <u>the world, in ancient times,</u> lush forests full of plants and animals.

    (A)   the world, in ancient times

    (B)   the world, being in ancient times

    (C)   the world were, in ancient times

    (D)   the world was, in ancient times

2. The land that is now Alaska, which was inhabited by the Tlingit tribe before being colonized by <u>Russia, sold by</u> Tsar Alexander II to the United States in 1867.

    (A)   Russia, sold by

    (B)   Russia, having been sold by

    (C)   Russia, was sold by

    (D)   Russia, to be sold by

3. Though the polecat looks like a weasel in appearance, <u>but has</u> more developed scent glands than a weasel.

    (A)   but has

    (B)   but it's having

    (C)   it is having

    (D)   it has

This page is intentionally left blank.
Content resumes on the next page.

Punctuation

In this chapter, you will determine whether and where commas are needed to set off or separate adjectives and parenthetical elements in sentences.

🎯 LEARNING TARGETS

1. Identify and punctuate equal adjectives in a sentence.

2. Locate and punctuate parenthetical elements in a sentence.

3. Use the comma placement inconsistencies among answer choices as a way to identify potential equal adjectives or parenthetical elements.

Warm-Up

Instructions

Complete the warm-up question. If time remains after you've finished, double-check your work.

Passage

(1) When schools of fish gather again after time apart, they will swim around each other while waving their fins and performing elaborate dances. **(2)** Stingrays have been seen, frolicking over fields of coral, twirling and flapping their wings, even when ample open ocean is readily available. **(3)** Some have argued that these kinds of behaviors show that fish can feel emotions like joy and delight.

(4) Even advocates for the argument that fish have feelings acknowledge that scientists can easily misidentify what they are seeing. **(5)** The shape of a fish's mouth makes it look like it is surprised; it looks that way even when it is excited or in danger. **(6)** Fish are social, communicating underwater using clicks and bubbles. **(7)** Feelings are challenging to understand even in humans, who have the ability to talk about their emotions.

(8) Many oceanographers who devote their time to studying fish behavior have argued that at least some fish, such as triggerfishes and eels, have strong feelings like the ones we experience as humans. **(9)** Other researchers are doubtful. **(10)** They argue that it has not yet been proven that fish feel emotion in any reliable, reproducible scientific experiments.

(11) Regardless, scientific consensus on the question of fish emotion is beginning to shift. **(12)** Many biologists have accepted that fish most likely have "primary" emotions such as fear or anger. **(13)** These responses seem to be found in most fish. **(14)** For instance, a zebrafish will avoid a part of the tank where it was once shocked even if the shock has been removed. **(15)** Additionally, scientists believe that feelings can be inferred from fishes' changes in activity and eye movement, or even from involuntary responses like scale shedding.

1. Which of the following is the best version of the underlined portion of sentence 2 (reproduced below)?

    Stingrays have been <u>seen, frolicking over fields of coral, twirling and flapping their wings,</u> even when ample open ocean is readily available.

    Ⓐ (as it is now)

    Ⓑ seen frolicking over fields of coral, twirling and flapping their wings,

    Ⓒ seen, frolicking over fields of coral, twirling and flapping their wings

    Ⓓ seen frolicking, over fields of coral, twirling and flapping their wings,

Groundwork

Instructions

Test each phrase to determine if a comma is needed to separate the adjectives. If a comma is needed, add it to the phrase.

Test #1: Swap the adjectives. Adjectives that can be swapped easily need a comma between them.

---

1. the adorable grumpy-looking viscacha

2. the ferocious hungry tiger

3. the graceful adult giraffe

4. the rare African parrot

EXERCISE B

Instructions

Test each phrase to determine if a comma is needed to separate the adjectives. If a comma is needed, add it to the phrase.

> **Test #2:** Add an "and." If the phrase still sounds correct with "and" between the adjectives, they should be separated by a comma.

5. the four large rattlesnakes

6. the falcon's lightweight aerodynamic body

7. the friendly Dalmatian puppies

8. the loud annoying frogs outside

Instructions
Refer to the following sentence as your teacher leads the discussion.

9.   The common <u>ostrich, the world's largest species of bird</u>, can sprint at speeds of over 40 mph.

Instructions
Determine whether the underlined portions in the passage contain a parenthetical element. If so, add commas to separate them from the rest of the sentence.

Passage
   (1) You may have heard that the pufferfish <u>a creature containing enough toxin to kill several dozen people at once</u> is considered a delicacy in Japan. **(2)** Chefs wishing to serve this fish <u>known in Japanese as *fugu* must undergo years of study</u> and pass a final examination that involves the live preparation and consumption of *fugu*. **(3)** *Fugu* is most commonly served raw <u>often with thin slices of meat arranged</u> into the shape of a flower, but it can also be fried, stewed, and grilled like any other fish. **(4)** Those brave enough to ingest it report <u>a delicate, savory, and surprisingly non-fishy taste</u>.

 **Application**

⊘ THE APPROACH

When you are challenged to correctly punctuate descriptive words and phrases on the test, use the following steps ...

1. Locate equal adjectives or parenthetical elements, if any appear.

2. Eliminate answer choices that contain incorrect comma placement.

10. Which version of the sentence below is punctuated correctly?

Cephalopods, a class of animals that includes octopuses and squids possess three separate hearts that pump oxygen-rich, blue-colored blood throughout their bodies.

Ⓐ (as it is now)

Ⓑ Cephalopods, a class of animals that includes octopuses and squids, possess three separate hearts that pump oxygen-rich, blue-colored blood throughout their bodies.

Ⓒ Cephalopods, a class of animals that includes octopuses and squids possess three separate hearts that pump oxygen-rich blue-colored blood throughout their bodies.

Ⓓ Cephalopods a class of animals that includes octopuses and squids possess three separate hearts that pump oxygen-rich, blue-colored blood throughout their bodies.

⊘ THE APPROACH

When you are challenged to correctly punctuate descriptive words and phrases on the test, use the following steps …

1. Locate equal adjectives or parenthetical elements, if any appear.

2. Eliminate answer choices that contain incorrect comma placement.

Passage

(1) Flamingos can survive in remarkably harsh climates. (2) Some flamingo species make their home in the barren frigid peaks of the Andes Mountains, while others reside in boiling hot springs. (3) Because flamingos can eat the toxic algae that grows in these remote and lifeless places, they have no trouble living there.

11. Which of the following is the best version of the underlined portion of sentence 2 (reproduced below)?

    Some flamingo species make their home in the barren frigid peaks of the Andes Mountains, while others reside in boiling hot springs.

    Ⓐ (as it is now)

    Ⓑ in the barren frigid peaks of the Andes Mountains, while others reside in boiling, hot springs

    Ⓒ in the barren, frigid peaks of the Andes Mountains, while others reside in boiling hot springs

    Ⓓ in the barren, frigid peaks of the Andes Mountains, while others reside in boiling, hot springs

 **Practice**

Instructions

Complete the practice set. If time remains after you've finished, double-check your work.

1. Which of the following is the best version of the underlined portion of the sentence below?

    Crocodiles have been <u>spotted, hovering near empty river banks, waiting and biding their time,</u> until some unsuspecting prey comes along for a drink of water.

    Ⓐ (as it is now)

    Ⓑ spotted hovering near empty river banks, waiting and biding their time,

    Ⓒ spotted, hovering near empty river banks, waiting and biding their time

    Ⓓ spotted hovering, near empty river banks, waiting and biding their time,

2. Which of the following is the best version of the underlined portion of the sentence below?

    Admiral Lavigne, the child of a <u>Belizean, immigrant mother and a Garifuna-speaking father, made it an official language, and offered native Garifuna speakers an agreement</u> to create peace.

    Ⓐ (as it is now)

    Ⓑ Belizean immigrant mother and a Garifuna-speaking father, made it an official language and offered native Garifuna speakers an agreement

    Ⓒ Belizean immigrant mother, and a Garifuna-speaking father, made it an official language and offered native Garifuna speakers an agreement,

    Ⓓ Belizean, immigrant mother and a Garifuna-speaking father, made it an official language, and offered native Garifuna speakers an agreement,

3. Which of the following is the best version of the underlined portion of the sentence below?

    Despite its dilapidated condition, the sculpture was a <u>widely, beloved</u> feature of the community.

    Ⓐ (as it is now)

    Ⓑ widely beloved,

    Ⓒ widely beloved

    Ⓓ widely, beloved

Wrap-Up

Instructions

Complete the wrap-up question. If time remains after you've finished, double-check your work.

Passage

(1) These days, Barcelona is the only city in Spain where a majority of the residents speak a regional language: Catalan. **(2)** It is taught to every child. **(3)** And to many adults, it is a source of cultural identity. **(4)** Barcelona differs substantially even from other autonomous regions in Spain like Basque Country, which has a majority Basque (rather than Spanish) population. **(5)** In Barcelona, Catalan and Castilian Spanish are both official languages. **(6)** Yet Catalan, alongside Spanish, is considered a primary language, spoken by 70 percent of Barcelonans. **(7)** In Basque Country, which also has two official languages, Basque is secondary to Spanish.

(8) Historians and anthropologists argue that the decline of this regional language dates back to the union of the Castile and Aragon crowns in the late 15th century. **(9)** However, as the monarchy sought to replace regional languages with Spanish, the territory that ultimately became Barcelona remained autonomous. **(10)** This helped preserve Catalan.

(11) Under General Francisco Franco, who ruled from 1936 to 1975, Catalan suffered. **(12)** General Franco, the son of a naval officer father and Spanish-speaking mother, made it a forbidden language and punished Catalan speakers with imprisonment for their disobedience. **(13)** Democratic government was established in the 1980s. **(14)** Then more actions were taken to preserve Catalan. **(15)** However, not everyone feels confident about Catalan's future, pointing to changes like the growing number of immigrants from Latin America, where Spanish is typically the dominant language, to Barcelona, where Catalan has the upper hand. **(16)** Whether Catalan can continue to grow, or at least hold on, in an increasingly migratory society within an ever-changing world remains an open question.

2. In context, which of the following is the best version of the underlined portion of sentence 12 (reproduced below)?

   General Franco, the son of a <u>naval officer father and Spanish-speaking mother, made it a forbidden language and punished Catalan speakers with imprisonment</u> for their disobedience.

   Ⓐ (as it is now)

   Ⓑ naval, officer father, and Spanish-speaking mother, made it a forbidden language, and punished Catalan speakers with imprisonment

   Ⓒ naval officer father, and Spanish-speaking mother, made it a forbidden language, and punished Catalan speakers with imprisonment,

   Ⓓ naval, officer father, and Spanish-speaking mother, made it a forbidden language, and punished Catalan speakers with imprisonment,

This page is intentionally left blank.
Content resumes on the next page.

Additional Phrases
and Clauses

In this chapter, you will learn how to utilize participial phrases and relative clauses to avoid sentence structure errors, such as fragments and comma splices.

🎯 LEARNING TARGETS

1. Identify redundancies and run-on sentences.

2. Recognize when modifications to a sentence structure result in a fragment or comma splice.

3. Construct and punctuate participial phrases and relative clauses.

 **Warm-Up**

Instructions

Complete the warm-up question. If time remains after you've finished, double-check your work.

1. By 1990, Nabisco's Oreos had become the most popular cookie in the United States, <u>they sold</u> millions of units.

   (A) they sold

   (B) they had sold

   (C) with selling

   (D) selling

Groundwork

EXERCISE A

Instructions
Locate two grammatically incorrect sentences in the following passage. Underline your answers.

Passage

(1) Did you know that the original drive-through window was invented for a very specific group of Americans? **(2)** Drive-throughs were designed to make life a little more convenient for U.S. military members, they were prohibited from wearing their uniforms in public. **(3)** That meant they'd have to go home and change clothes before heading out for a burger. **(4)** But in 1975, one McDonald's owner decided to do something that created a kind of loophole. **(5)** He cut a hole in the side of his building, he had allowing soldiers to drive up in their cars and order food without breaking any rules.

EXERCISE B

Instructions
Determine which solution best completes the sentence. Circle your answer.

(2) Drive-throughs were designed to make life a little more convenient for U.S. military members, they were prohibited from wearing their uniforms in public.

To correct the error in this sentence …

… remove the comma.

… change "they were prohibited" to "prohibiting."

… change "they" to "who."

EXERCISE C

Instructions

Determine which solution best completes the sentence. Circle your answer.

(5) He cut a hole in the side of his building, he had allowing soldiers to drive up in their cars and order food without breaking any rules.

To correct the error in this sentence …

… change "he" to "who."

… change "he" to "him."

… remove "he had" from the sentence.

Application

⊘ THE APPROACH

When you are asked to find the appropriate phrase and clause, use these steps ...

1. Determine if the underlined portion contains the main verb of the sentence.
2. If it <u>does</u>, eliminate answer choices that contain inappropriate verbs.
3. If it <u>doesn't</u>, eliminate answers that create run-ons, comma splices, or fragments.
4. If more than one answer remains, eliminate answers that *sound* wrong.

1. The crew of <u>astronauts, they were studying</u> the effects of weightlessness on the human heart.

   (A) astronauts, they were studying

   (B) astronauts studied

   (C) astronauts to have studied

   (D) astronauts, who were studying

⊘ THE APPROACH

When you are asked to find the appropriate phrase and clause, use these steps ...

1. Determine if the underlined portion contains the main verb of the sentence.
2. If it <u>does</u>, eliminate answer choices that contain inappropriate verbs.
3. If it <u>doesn't</u>, eliminate answers that create run-ons, comma splices, or fragments.
4. If more than one answer remains, eliminate answers that *sound* wrong.

2. By 1969, Union Pacific had become the most successful rail company in the United States, <u>they laid</u> 800 miles of rail line.

    Ⓐ they laid
    Ⓑ with laid
    Ⓒ they had laid
    Ⓓ laying

 **Practice**

Instructions

Complete the practice set. If time remains after you've finished, double-check your work.

1. The children thought that their father was being <u>serious when he told</u> them that the word "gullible" is not in the dictionary.

    (A) serious when he told

    (B) serious he told

    (C) serious, he telling

    (D) serious him telling

2. The opera singer utterly amazed the <u>audience they cheered</u> for an encore and threw flowers for an entire minute after the last song.

    (A) audience they cheered

    (B) audience to cheer

    (C) audience, cheering

    (D) audience, who cheered

3. <u>It had just been removed from the freezer</u> the casserole was nearly frozen solid.

    (A) It had just been removed from the freezer

    (B) Just been removed from the freezer and

    (C) Having just been removed from the freezer,

    (D) Had just been removed from the freezer,

Wrap-Up

Instructions
Complete the wrap-up question. If time remains after you've finished, double-check your work.

2. The party of <u>Dwarves, they were determined</u> to reclaim the right to their homeland, fought bravely to defend the Lonely Mountain from the Orcs and the Wargs.

   Ⓐ Dwarves, they were determined

   Ⓑ Dwarves determining

   Ⓒ Dwarves to have determined

   Ⓓ Dwarves, who were determined

This page is intentionally left blank.
Content resumes on the next page.

Essay Orientation

In this chapter, you will become familiar with the characteristics and grading standards of the TSIA2 Essay section.

Groundwork

Instructions

Refer to the following table as your teacher leads the discussion.

Subject	Passing Score
English Language Arts and Reading	
Multiple Choice	945+
Essay*	5+
Mathematics	
Multiple Choice	950+

How Is the Essay Scored?

The essay is scored according to your performance in the following areas:

- **Purpose and Focus:** the essay remains on topic and has a clear main idea.
- **Organization and Structure:** the essay's ideas are well-organized, typically through paragraphs.
- **Development and Support:** evidence is provided to support the main idea of the essay.
- **Sentence Variety and Style:** the essay contains correct and varied sentence structures, along with a formal tone and appropriate vocabulary use.
- **Mechanical Conventions:** the essay is written using correct grammar and punctuation.
- **Critical Thinking:** there is a logical progression of ideas through the essay.

EXERCISE A

Instructions
Review the TSIA2 Essay grading standard and circle the score an essay with that characteristic would earn on the test.

1. Presents a vague or limited point of view on the issue

    2   or   6

2. May stray from the audience and purpose but is able to refocus

    5   or   8

3. Exhibits skillful use of language, using a varied, accurate, and apt vocabulary

    5   or   8

4. Demonstrates adequate variety in sentence structure

    3   or   6

5. Provides inappropriate or insufficient examples, reasons, or other evidence to support its position

    3   or   5

6. Organizes ideas ineffectively, demonstrating a problematic progression of ideas

    2   or   6

Instructions
Refer to the following instructions as your teacher leads the discussion.

The essay gives you an opportunity to show how effectively you can develop and express your ideas in writing.

You will first read a short passage and an assignment question that are focused on an important issue. You will then write an essay in which you develop your own point of view on the issue. You should support your position with appropriate reasoning and examples. The position you take will not influence your score.

Your essay will be given a holistic score that represents how clearly and effectively you expressed your position. The following six characteristics of writing will be considered.

- **Purpose and Focus** - The extent to which you present information in a unified and coherent manner, clearly addressing the issue.
- **Organization and Structure** - The extent to which you order and connect ideas.
- **Development and Support** - The extent to which you develop and support ideas.
- **Sentence Variety and Style** - The extent to which you craft sentences and paragraphs demonstrating control of vocabulary, voice, and structure.
- **Mechanical Conventions** - The extent to which you express ideas using standard written English.
- **Critical Thinking** - The extent to which you communicate a point of view and demonstrate reasoned relationships among ideas.

Scores on WritePlacer range from 1 to 8. An essay will be given a score of zero if it is too short to be evaluated, written on a topic other than the one presented, or written in a language other than English.

PLEASE NOTE: The WritePlacer essay must be completed in one sitting. You will not be allowed to stop and finish your essay later. Please see your Proctor if you have questions regarding timing.

EXERCISE B

Instructions
Review the following as your teacher leads the discussion.

Passage
"I learned that courage was not the absence of fear, but the triumph over it. The brave man is not he who does not feel afraid, but he who conquers that fear."

Adapted from Nelson Mandela, *Long Walk to Freedom*

Assignment
Are we in control of our fears?

Plan and write a multiparagraph essay (300–600 words) in which you develop your point of view on the above question. Support your position with reasoning and examples taken from your reading, studies, experience, or observations.

Application

Instructions

Sequence the steps for writing your TSIA2 essay by placing the numbers 1–6 in the space provided.

⊘ THE APPROACH

When you reach the Essay section of the TSIA2, follow these steps ...

_____ Write the introduction.

_____ Write the conclusion.

_____ Decide your opinion.

_____ Brainstorm and outline.

_____ Write two body paragraphs.

_____ Review your essay.

Brainstorming and Pre-Writing

In this chapter, you will learn a variety of techniques for gathering and selecting relevant ideas that will support your argument. In addition, you will learn how to organize ideas into a standard essay outline.

🎯 LEARNING TARGETS

1. Evaluate and respond to the essay prompt of the TSIA2.

2. Gather and select examples to most effectively support your opinion.

3. Organize your ideas into an outline in order to create a standard essay structure.

EXERCISE A

Instructions

Fill in the following diagram using word association.

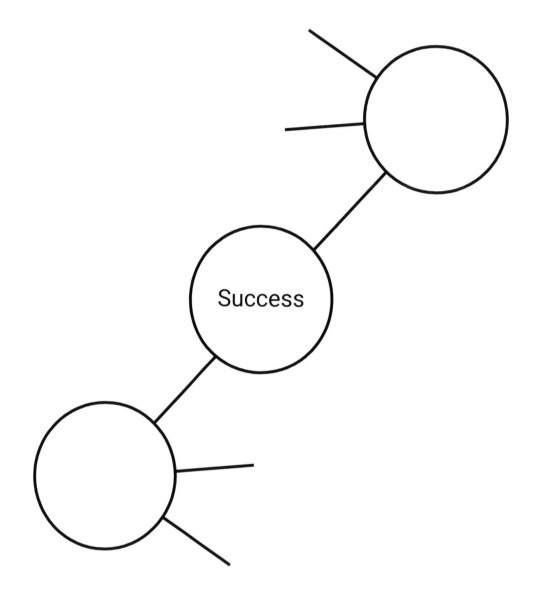

EXERCISE B

Instructions
Refer to the following as the teacher leads the discussion.

Passage
"I learned that courage was not the absence of fear, but the triumph over it. The brave man is not he who does not feel afraid, but he who conquers that fear."

Adapted from Nelson Mandela, *Long Walk to Freedom*

Assignment
Are we in control of our fears?

Plan and write a multiparagraph essay (300–600 words) in which you develop your point of view on the above question. Support your position with reasoning and examples taken from your reading, studies, experience, or observations.

1. Circle your response to the question posed in the Assignment: *Are we in control of our fears?*

         Yes   No

EXERCISE C >

Instructions

Use your response to the question posed in the Assignment to practice brainstorming.

2. Brainstorm some ideas in the space below. Write down at least 3 examples you could use in your essay to support your opinion.

_____

_____

_____

_____

_____

_____

_____

_____

_____

_____

_____

_____

Application

⊘ THE APPROACH

When you begin working on your essay during the TSIA2, you should ...

1. Review the Passage and respond to the question in the Assignment.
2. Brainstorm and select two examples to support your response.
3. Construct an outline to organize your ideas.

Instructions

Fill in the blanks as the teacher leads the discussion.

CREATE AN OUTLINE

Introduction Paragraph

1. _____

2. _____

3. _____

Body Paragraph 1

1. _____

2. _____

Body Paragraph 2

1. _____

2. _____

Conclusion Paragraph

1. _____

2. _____

This page is intentionally left blank.
Content resumes on the next page.

Writing the Introduction

In this chapter, you will be introduced to the three main elements of an introduction paragraph. Additionally, you will evaluate and use strategies to draft an opening hook, preview, and thesis statement.

🎯 LEARNING TARGETS

1. Identify and define the three main elements of an introduction paragraph.

2. Evaluate potential strategies for writing an opening hook.

3. Draft an opening hook, preview, and thesis statement in response to a TSIA2-style essay prompt.

Groundwork

EXERCISE A

Instructions
Fill in the following definitions as your teacher leads the discussion.

1. Hook: _____

2. Preview: _____

3. Thesis: _____

EXERCISE B

Instructions

Evaluate each of the following strategies for writing a hook. Place a check mark next to the ones you think are effective options.

_____   Ask a relevant question.

_____   Use at least three exclamation points at the end of your sentence.

_____   Make an interesting or strong statement about the topic.

_____   Write a confusing sentence so that the reader has to continue reading to figure out what you meant.

_____   Describe a relevant image or scene.

EXERCISE C >

Instructions
Refer to the following as the teacher leads the discussion.

Passage
"I learned that courage was not the absence of fear, but the triumph over it. The brave man is not he who does not feel afraid, but he who conquers that fear."

Adapted from Nelson Mandela, *Long Walk to Freedom*

Assignment
Are we in control of our fears?

Plan and write a multiparagraph essay (300–600 words) in which you develop your point of view on the above question. Support your position with reasoning and examples taken from your reading, studies, experience, or observations.

4. Which of the following is the *most* effective preview? Circle your answer.

    A. Can we ever be without fear? No. Fear is a part of our lives.

    B. There are many examples from history, literature, and film that show characters who are put in difficult situations in which they have to face their fears.

    C. Nour and Mulan, strong fictional characters, both face challenging moments that make them fearful, but they overcome their fears and save those they love.

EXERCISE D

Instructions
Determine whether each statement is a fact or an opinion. Circle your answers.

5. The summer heat in southern states like Texas and Arizona can cause severe dehydration if a person does not take the necessary precautions.

        Fact   Opinion

6. The most worthwhile part of any NFL Super Bowl is the commercials because they are the most entertaining.

        Fact   Opinion

EXERCISE E

Instructions
Circle the key words in the question as your teacher leads the discussion.

7. Are we in control of our fears?

8. Does wealth make us happy?

9. Is adversity a potentially good motivator?

Application

✓ THE APPROACH

When writing the introduction paragraph for your essay during the TSIA2 ...

1. Craft an attention-grabbing hook.

2. Mention the subject of your two examples as a preview.

3. Draft a thesis that flows from the preview, responds to the assignment's question, and states your opinion clearly.

Passage
"I learned that courage was not the absence of fear, but the triumph over it. The brave man is not he who does not feel afraid, but he who conquers that fear."

Adapted from Nelson Mandela, *Long Walk to Freedom*

Assignment
Are we in control of our fears?

Plan and write a multiparagraph essay (300–600 words) in which you develop your point of view on the above question. Support your position with reasoning and examples taken from your reading, studies, experience, or observations.

Instructions
Refer to the following example as your teacher leads the discussion.

We have two choices when we are afraid: we can run and hide or we can stand and face our fears. Nour and Mulan, strong fictional characters, both face challenging moments that make them fearful, but they overcome their fears and save those they love. These characters prove that even though we may be afraid, we are in control of our fears.

⊘ THE APPROACH

When writing the introduction paragraph for your essay during the TSIA2 ...

1. Craft an attention-grabbing hook.

2. Mention the subject of your two examples as a preview.

3. Draft a thesis that flows from the preview, responds to the assignment's question, and states your opinion clearly.

Passage

"I learned that courage was not the absence of fear, but the triumph over it. The brave man is not he who does not feel afraid, but he who conquers that fear."

Adapted from Nelson Mandela, *Long Walk to Freedom*

Assignment

Are we in control of our fears?

Plan and write a multiparagraph essay (300–600 words) in which you develop your point of view on the above question. Support your position with reasoning and examples taken from your reading, studies, experience, or observations.

Instructions

Draft your introduction paragraph here:

_____

_____

_____

_____

_____

Instructions

Review your partner's introduction paragraph on the previous page. Then, provide feedback in the space below.

Positive: _____

_____

_____

_____

_____

_____

Constructive: _____

_____

_____

_____

_____

_____

This page is intentionally left blank.
Content resumes on the next page.

Developing Body Paragraphs

In this chapter, you will learn how to expand your introductory paragraph into two well-formed body paragraphs. You will also develop skills to transition between body paragraphs.

🎯 LEARNING TARGETS

1. Identify and define the main elements of a body paragraph.

2. Learn strategies to provide support for a thesis statement.

3. Draft two body paragraphs in response to a TSIA2-style essay prompt.

Groundwork

EXERCISE A

Instructions

Review the following topic sentence as your teacher leads the discussion.

> *The love we have for our family can give us the courage to face our fear and overcome it.*

Topic Sentence for Body Paragraph #1:

_____

_____

_____

_____

_____

EXERCISE B

Instructions

Refer to the following example summaries as your teacher leads the discussion. Then, write your own summary for your first body paragraph.

Option 1

> The main character, a girl who is in a country in the Middle East, dives in the water at some point during the story to save her sister from a terrible fate.

Option 2

> Nour, an 11-year-old girl in the novel *The Map of Salt and Stars*, has long been afraid of the water because of a traumatic incident when she was little and has not learned how to swim since. She also has a little sister, Zahra. They haven't always had the best relationship. In fact, it's often been really turbulent at times. After her father dies of cancer, Nour's mother decides to make a change. She moves them from their home in New York back to Syria, which isn't what it used to be. One day, Nour sees her sister, Zahra, struggling in the dark and churning sea. She doesn't hesitate and dives in, overcoming her fear of the water and saving her sister all in one fell swoop.

Option 3

> Nour, the main character in the novel *The Map of Salt and Stars*, not only doesn't know how to swim but has always feared the water. However, when she sees her sister, Zahra, struggling in the sea, Nour dives in without hesitation and pulls her to safety.

Example Summary for Body Paragraph #1:

_____

_____

_____

_____

_____

_____

EXERCISE C

Instructions

Review the following body paragraph as your teacher leads the discussion.

---

(1) The love we have for our family can give us the courage to face our fear and overcome it. **(2)** Nour, the main character in the novel *The Map of Salt and Stars*, not only doesn't know how to swim but has always feared the water. **(3)** However, when she sees her sister, Zahra, struggling in the sea, Nour dives in without hesitation and pulls her to safety. **(4)** This shows that Nour's love for her sister is stronger than her fear of water. **(5)** Because of her love for Zahra, Nour conquers her fear of the water and is able to save her sister. **(6)** Without that compelling force, Nour may not have been able to gather the courage to dive into the sea.

Commentary for Body Paragraph #1:

_____

_____

_____

_____

_____

_____

Application

✓ THE APPROACH

When writing a body paragraph for your essay during the TSIA2 ...

1. Develop a clear topic sentence.
2. Write 2–3 sentences that summarize your example.
3. Write 2–3 sentences of supporting commentary to explain how your example proves your thesis.

Passage

"I learned that courage was not the absence of fear, but the triumph over it. The brave man is not he who does not feel afraid, but he who conquers that fear."

Adapted from Nelson Mandela, *Long Walk to Freedom*

Assignment

Are we in control of our fears?

Plan and write a multiparagraph essay (300–600 words) in which you develop your point of view on the above question. Support your position with reasoning and examples taken from your reading, studies, experiences, or observations.

Draft your second paragraph here. Be sure to include a transition at the start of your topic sentence.

_____

_____

_____

_____

_____

_____

_____

_____

⊘ THE APPROACH

When writing a body paragraph for your essay during the TSIA2 ...

1. Develop a clear topic sentence.
2. Write 2–3 sentences that summarize your example.
3. Write 2–3 sentences of supporting commentary to explain how your example proves your thesis.

Instructions
Review your partner's second body paragraph on the previous page. Then, provide feedback in the space provided.

Positive:

_____

_____

_____

_____

_____

Constructive:

_____

_____

_____

_____

_____

35

Writing the Conclusion

In this chapter, you will learn how to craft a concluding paragraph that will recap the main point of your essay and create a connection with the reader.

🎯 LEARNING TARGETS

1. Develop an opening sentence for a conclusion that effectively restates the thesis.

2. Review strategies used to form a connection with readers.

3. Draft a conclusion paragraph.

 **Groundwork**

EXERCISE A

Instructions
Underline the thesis statement in the example introduction paragraph. Then, place a check mark next to the options that would make an effective opening sentence for the conclusion paragraph.

Introduction Paragraph
We have two choices when we are afraid: we can run and hide or we can stand and face our fear. Nour and Mulan, strong fictional characters, both face challenging moments that make them fearful, but they overcome their fears and save those they love. These characters prove that even though we may be afraid, we are in control of our fears.

1. _____ These characters prove that even though we may be afraid, we are in control of our fears.

2. _____ There is much to fear in this world, but at the end of the day, we must face it or perish.

3. _____ Nour and Mulan were able to conquer their fear because of special circumstances, but most of us are not able to do that because we are riddled with uncertainty.

4. _____ Although they encountered dangerous situations, Nour and Mulan put the lives of others before themselves and show that we are in control of our fear.

Instructions

Use the space provided to develop the first sentence of your conclusion paragraph.

1. Rewrite your thesis:

_____

_____

_____

_____

_____

_____

_____

2. Write the first sentence of your conclusion paragraph:

_____

_____

_____

_____

_____

_____

_____

EXERCISE C

Instructions

Match each strategy to its definition by writing the corresponding letter in the space provided.

1. _____ So What?

2. _____ Anticipating the Objection

3. _____ Powerful Words

A. Provide an opposing argument and explain why it's incorrect.

B. Use strong, descriptive words that evoke an emotional response from the reader.

C. Explain why the topic should be important to the reader.

Application

⊘ THE APPROACH

When you draft the conclusion paragraph for your essay during the TSIA2, use these steps ...

1. Open the paragraph with a restatement of your thesis.
2. Close the paragraph with a connection with the reader.

Conclusion Paragraph Draft:

_____

_____

_____

_____

_____

_____

_____

_____

_____

_____

_____

_____

_____

_____

⊘ THE APPROACH

When you draft the conclusion paragraph for your essay during the TSIA2, use these steps ...

1. Open the paragraph with a restatement of your thesis.
2. Close the paragraph with a connection with the reader.

Instructions

In the space provided, give your peer feedback on their conclusion paragraph.

Positive:

_____

_____

_____

_____

_____

Constructive:

_____

_____

_____

_____

_____

Revising and Editing

In this chapter, you will learn strategies for revising and editing your essay submission for the TSIA2.

Groundwork

EXERCISE A

Instructions
Refer to the following as the teacher leads the discussion.

Passage
"I learned that courage was not the absence of fear, but the triumph over it. The brave man is not he who does not feel afraid, but he who conquers that fear."

Adapted from Nelson Mandela, *Long Walk to Freedom*

Assignment
Are we in control of our fears?

Plan and write a multiparagraph essay (300–600 words) in which you develop your point of view on the above question. Support your position with reasoning and examples taken from your reading, studies, experience, or observations.

> We have two choices when we are afraid: we can run and hide or we can stand and face our fear. Nour and Mulan, strong fictional characters, both face challenging moments that make them fearful, but they overcome their fears and save those they love. These characters prove that even though we may be afraid, we are in control of our fears.
> The love we have for our family can give us the courage to face our fear and overcome it. Nour, the main character in *The Map of Salt and Stars*, not only doesn't know how to swim but has always feared the water. However, when she sees her sister, Zahra, struggling in the sea, Nour dives in without hesitation and pulls her to safety. This shows that Nour's love for her sister is stronger than her fear of water. Because of her love for Zahra, Nour conquers her fear of the water and is able to save her sister. Without that compelling force, Nour may not have been able to gather the courage to dive into the sea.

Word Count: 487

EXERCISE B

Instructions

Review the following passage. Cross out or replace any unnecessary words to reduce the word count.

Passage

(1) I really and truly love fostering animals for the shelter. **(2)** It is very satisfying to know that I am helping animals build incredibly strong bonds with humans again. **(3)** On the other hand, though, I find it difficult to let go of some fosters and sometimes end up adopting them! **(4)** My dog, Summer, is one of those. **(5)** Her sweet, delightful, charming, friendly nature won me over.

EXERCISE C

Instructions
Review the following essay and identify three places where more information could be added.

Passage
Perhaps humankind's greatest mystery is the purpose of life. Why do humans exist? And what are they meant to do with their time on this planet? While many might argue that every human should spend their life in pursuit of some goal or level of greatness, it is equally possible that the purpose of life is to live in a manner that leads to a feeling of contentment. This is evident in the story of Ove, an elderly gentleman, along with Mrs. Dalloway and her attempts to throw the perfect dinner party. It is in the ordinary and mundane that humans will find the most happiness and greatest meaning in life.

In the story of *A Man Called Ove*, a young couple and their two daughters move into a home next to a curmudgeon of a man named Ove. He is everything you'd expect in a cranky old neighbor. He hollers, scoffs, and absolutely never smiles. As his neighbors' antics irritate him, he reacts with annoyance and guidance. By helping the new couple in many ways, Ove and his new neighbors experience great joy.

Mrs. Dalloway is another prime example of finding happiness in living a life doing things that one loves. She spends her time preparing for and ultimately succeeding at planning an exceptional dinner party. Her story is average, potentially boring even. Despite being the story of a housewife planning and preparing for a party, the story has become a classic.

Word Count: 243

EXERCISE D

Instructions

Identify and correct the four grammar, punctuation, and spelling errors that appear in the following essay.

> We have two choices when we are afraid: we can run nad hide or we can stand and face our fear. Nour and Mulan, strong fictional characters, both face challenging moments that make them fearful, but they overcome their fears and save those they love.
>
> The love we have, for our family can give us courage to face our fear and overcome it. Nour, the the main character in the novel The Map of Salt and Stars not only doesn't know how to swim but has always feared the water. However, when she sees her sister Zahra struggling in the sea, Nour dives in without hesitation and pulls her to safety. This shows that Nour's love for her sister is stronger than her fear of water. Because of her love for Zahra. Nour conquers her fear of the water and is able to save her sister. Without that compelling force, Nour may not have been able to gather the courage needed to dive into the sea.

Application

⊘ THE APPROACH

When you are finished drafting your essay during the TSIA2, use these steps ...

1. Take a mental break.
2. Add or cut words to ensure the essay is between 300 and 600 words.
3. Review the essay to check for common grammar, punctuation, and spelling errors.

Instructions

Collect your writing from the previous essay chapters into a single written piece. You should either rewrite the essay in your workbook or type your essay into a text document on the computer. As you collect the pieces of your essay, check the word count to ensure your work fits within the 300–600 limit of the TSIA2.

Essay:

Essay (Continued):

_____

_____

_____

_____

_____

_____

_____

_____

_____

_____

_____

_____

_____

_____

⊘ THE APPROACH

When you are finished drafting your essay during the TSIA2, use these steps ...

1. Take a mental break.

2. Add or cut words to ensure the essay is between 300 and 600 words.

3. Review the essay to check for common grammar, punctuation, and spelling errors.

Proofreading Strategies

✓ Start at the bottom and work your way up.

✓ Focus on one error type at a time.

✓ Read the sentence under your breath to listen for mistakes.

✓ Highlight one line at a time with your cursor to improve focus.

⊘ THE APPROACH

When you are finished drafting your essay during the TSIA2, use these steps ...

1. Take a mental break.
2. Add or cut words to ensure the essay is between 300 and 600 words.
3. Review the essay to check for common grammar, punctuation, and spelling errors.

Instructions

Proofread your essay. Note any mistakes you correct in the space provided.

1. _____

2. _____

3. _____

4. _____

5. _____

6. _____

7. _____

8. _____

9. _____

10. _____

This page is intentionally left blank.
Content resumes on the next page.

Practice Prompts

In this chapter, you will practice constructing standardized essays using prompts similar to what they will see on the TSIA2.

🎯 LEARNING TARGETS

1. Utilize effective pre-writing strategies.

2. Draft 4-paragraph essays that adhere to a standardized structure.

3. Revise an essay to ensure it falls within the word limit.

4. Identify errors in an essay using standard English conventions.

Groundwork

EXERCISE A

Instructions
Review the writing prompt. Then, decide which side of the argument you want to support. Place a check mark next to your selection.

Passage
All of the great social justice advances that we ever had in this country have come not from people with big titles and not from people at the top, but just from everyday people getting together saying, "Enough is enough. I'm going to change this, and I'm going to get involved, and I am going to be engaged."

Adapted from Nina Turner, "Nina Turner at the Women's Convention"

Assignment
Who has the greatest potential to set social change into motion: someone with a high social status or an individual who lacks power but has a great amount of determination?

Plan and write a multiparagraph essay (between 300 and 600 words) in which you explain your opinion about the above question. Support your ideas with a clear argument and examples from media, books, current events, or personal experiences.

1. Which side of the argument do you plan to take?

   _____ Someone with a high social status has the most potential to inspire social change.

   _____ An individual with no power but a lot of determination has the most potential to inspire social change.

EXERCISE B

Instructions

Brainstorm examples you can use to support your essay's central argument.

_____

_____

_____

_____

_____

_____

_____

_____

_____

_____

_____

_____

_____

_____

_____

_____

_____

_____

_____

EXERCISE C

Instructions

Use the provided structure to create an outline for your essay. You do not need to use complete sentences.

Introduction

Hook: _____

Preview: _____

Preview: _____

Body Paragraph 1

Example: _____

Significance: _____

Body Paragraph 2

Example: _____

Significance: _____

Conclusion

Thesis Restatement: _____

Connection to the Reader: _____

EXERCISE D

Instructions
Use the space provided to draft your essay.

Introduction   Word Count _____

_____

_____

_____

_____

First Body Paragraph   Word Count _____

_____

_____

_____

_____

Second Body Paragraph   Word Count: _____

_____

_____

_____

_____

Conclusion   Word Count: _____

_____

_____

_____

_____

Total Word Count: _____

EXERCISE E

Instructions
Review your essay on the previous page and note three errors you discovered while revising and editing.

Errors Discovered

1. _____

2. _____

3. _____

Application

⊘ THE APPROACH

When writing your essay for the TSIA2, follow these steps ...

1. Read the prompt and decide your stance.
2. Brainstorm ideas and organize them into an outline.
3. Draft your introduction, two body paragraphs, and conclusion.
4. Revise and edit.

Passage

1. Competition brings out the best in products and industry, and yet, it seems to draw out the absolute worst in people.

Adapted from David Sarnoff

2. Competition is one of the most important drivers of innovation because you have to stay in the race. You have to think of something new, and if you don't, well, of course you bow out.

Adapted from Margrethe Vestager

Assignment

In today's world, is competition a healthy motivation or a driving force that encourages pride, selfishness, and greed?

Plan and write a multiparagraph essay (between 300 and 600 words) in which you explain your opinion about the above question. Support your ideas with a clear argument and examples from media, books, current events, or personal experiences.

Instructions
Use the space provided to draft your essay.

Introduction   Word Count _____

_____

_____

_____

_____

First Body Paragraph   Word Count _____

_____

_____

_____

_____

Second Body Paragraph   Word Count _____

_____

_____

_____

_____

Conclusion   Word Count _____

_____

_____

_____

_____

Total Word Count: _____

⊘ THE APPROACH

When writing your essay for the TSIA2, follow these steps …

1. Read the prompt and decide your stance.
2. Brainstorm ideas and organize them into an outline.
3. Draft your introduction, two body paragraphs, and conclusion.
4. Revise and edit.

Passage

To be hopeful in bad times is not just foolishly romantic. It is based on the fact that human history is a history not only of cruelty, but also of compassion, sacrifice, courage, kindness. What we choose to emphasize in this complex history will determine our lives. If we see only the worst, it destroys our capacity to do something. If we remember those times and places—and there are so many—where people have behaved magnificently, this gives us the energy to act, and at least the possibility of sending this spinning top of a world in a different direction.

Adapted from Howard Zinn, *A Marvelous Victory*

Assignment

Is it better to look at the world from an optimistic viewpoint, or is it more advantageous to expect things to go wrong?

Plan and write a multiparagraph essay (between 300 and 600 words) in which you explain your opinion about the above question. Support your ideas with a clear argument and examples from media, books, current events, or personal experiences.

Instructions
Use the space provided to draft your essay.

Introduction   Word Count _____

_____

_____

_____

_____

First Body Paragraph   Word Count _____

_____

_____

_____

_____

Second Body Paragraph   Word Count _____

_____

_____

_____

_____

Conclusion   Word Count _____

_____

_____

_____

_____

_____

Total Word Count: _____

Instructions

In this section, review your writing and take notes on your strengths and weaknesses.

I do these things really well:

1. _____

2. _____

3. _____

I should double-check these things on test day:

1. _____

2. _____

3. _____

This page is intentionally left blank.
Content resumes on the next page.

Contributors

Director of Curriculum
Stephanie Constantino

Publisher
Craig Gehring

Chief Academic Officer
Oliver Pope

Layout and Design Lead
Jeff Garrett

Quality Control Team Lead
Allison Eskind

Item Lead
Peter Franco

Senior Proofreader
AndreAnna McLean

Cover Design
Nicole St. Pierre

Content Creation
Anne Delatte
Amelia Emery
Sandy Fahringer
Lee Hair
Lana Johnson
Nick Pilewski
Lauren Pope
Daniel Romero
Michelle Wolf

Item Creation
Eric Manuel
Megan Reynolds
Daniel Romero
Zora Rush
Theresa Schlafly
Minrose Strausman
Luke Switzer

Proofreaders
Juan Aponte
Lauren Brecht
Andrea Broussard
Andrea Cole
Ainsley Davis
Cassandra Galentine
Ginny Gillikin
Alison Hertz
May Lane
Lauren Miklovic
Llaina Rash
Luke Switzer
Maghie Zeigler

Layout and Graphics
Kayla Manuel
Hope Oswald
Amanda Pfeil
Jaye Pratt

Subject Matter Experts
Destiny Blue
Lauren Brecht
Colin Brinkerhoff
Kerri Denholm
Amelia Emery
Lee Hair
Eric Manuel
Rebecca Pickens
Nick Pilewski
Daniel Romero
Theresa Schlafly
Stephanie Stewart
Luke Switzer
Mark Teel

Slide Designers
Lisa Halem
Karen Kilpatrick
June Manuel
Hope Oswald
Luke Switzer

Made in the USA
Middletown, DE
06 September 2022